3/30/16

Jarrod!

Thank you! for your

leadership + friendship!

CTW!

Every Good Endeavor

REDEEMER

Every Good Endeavor

Connecting Your Work to God's Work

TIMOTHY KELLER

with Katherine Leary Alsdorf

DUTTON

DUTTON
Published by Penguin Group (USA) Inc.
375 Hudson Street, New York, New York 10014, USA
Penguin Group (Canada), 90 Eglinton Avenue East, Suite 700, Toronto, Ontario M4P 2Y3,
Canada (a division of Pearson Penguin Canada Inc.); Penguin Books Ltd, 80 Strand, London
WC2R 0RL, England; Penguin Ireland, 25 St Stephen's Green, Dublin 2, Ireland (a division of
Penguin Books Ltd); Penguin Group (Australia), 707 Collins St., Melbourne, Victoria 3008,
Australia (a division of Pearson Australia Group Pty Ltd); Penguin Books India Pvt Ltd, 11
Community Centre, Panchsheel Park, New Delhi–110 017, India; Penguin Group (NZ),
67 Apollo Drive, Rosedale, Auckland 0632, New Zealand (a division of Pearson New Zealand Ltd);
Penguin Books, Rosebank Office Park, 181 Jan Smuts Avenue, Parktown North 2193,
South Africa; Penguin China, B7 Jiaming Center, 27 East Third Ring Road North,
Chaoyang District, Beijing 100020, China

Penguin Books Ltd, Registered Offices: 80 Strand, London WC2R 0RL, England

Published by Dutton, a member of Penguin Group (USA) Inc.

First printing, November 2012
1   3   5   7   9   10   8   6   4   2

Some names and identifying characteristics have been changed to protect the privacy of the
individuals involved.

All Bible references are from the New International Version (NIV), except where noted.

Figure on page 250 copyright © Redeemer Presbyterian Church

REGISTERED TRADEMARK—MARCA REGISTRADA

LIBRARY OF CONGRESS CATALOGING-IN-PUBLICATION DATA
has been applied for.

ISBN 978-0-525-95270-1

Printed in the United States of America
Set in ITC Galliard Std.
Designed by Leonard Telesca

While the author has made every effort to provide accurate telephone numbers, Internet addresses,
and other contact information at the time of publication, neither the publisher nor the author
assumes any responsibility for errors or for changes that occur after publication. Further, publisher
does not have any control over and does not assume any responsibility for author or third-party
websites or their content.

To the staff and volunteer leaders of Redeemer's Center for Faith & Work, who have helped our congregation see that the gospel really does change everything.

CONTENTS

Contents

During the year 1957, I experienced, by the grace of God, a spiritual awakening which was to lead me to a richer, fuller, more productive life. At that time, in gratitude, I humbly asked to be given the means and privilege to make others happy through music. I feel this has been granted through His grace. ALL PRAISE TO GOD. . . .

This album is a humble offering to Him. An attempt to say "THANK YOU GOD" through our work, even as we do in our hearts and with our tongues. May He help and strengthen all men in every good endeavor.

—John Coltrane, excerpt, liner notes to *A Love Supreme*

FOREWORD

In 1989 a colleague prodded me to come to her church—a
start-up in Manhattan called Redeemer Presbyterian Church.
I had been thoroughly inoculated against church years before,
having determined that the religion of my family's church was
more form than substance and that any leanings I might have had
in that direction were easily overcome by enlightened thinking.
But Redeemer caught my attention in a few ways: The pastor was
intelligent and talked like a normal person, he seemed to take the
Bible seriously, and he tried to apply it to parts of life that were
important to me—like my work.

A few years later I decided it was time to commit to faith and "give
my life" to the truth and promises of the Bible. I was worried, I admit, that this commitment might put an end to my career ambitions
and material comforts because, in fact, two of my brothers who had
become Christians had been "called" to be missionaries overseas.
One lived in rural Africa without running water or electricity. If I was
going to really put God first I had to be open to him calling me to
serve him *anywhere*. And he did. A few weeks after my decision, I was
stunned by the sudden illness of my boss, the CEO—and his request
that I take over leadership of the company. Given the circumstances,
I took it as an indication from God that he wanted me to play my part
not in the third world but in the world of business.

For the next decade, I served in executive leadership in several entrepreneurial tech companies in New York City, Europe, and Silicon Valley. In each job and each day I wrestled with what it means to be "called to serve God" as a leader in business. Redeemer and its senior pastor, Tim Keller, had given me good grounding. I'd learned that I was supposed to be changed by the gospel of Jesus Christ and therefore be "used by God" in my relationships with others, and maybe even be distinctive in the way I led companies. Nice concepts, but what did they look like in practice?

The models were few and often seemed remnants of an age when most of America went to church. One CEO would share that he kept a Bible on his desk and that occasionally someone in the company would ask about it. Another prayed and the company thrived. Many viewed their corporate jobs primarily as a means to make lots of money to give away to charities and organizations they cared about. When I asked pastors and businesspeople how their faith related to their work, they often answered that a Christian's primary, if not sole, mission in the workplace was to evangelize those with whom they worked. But most businesspeople would quickly add that evangelism was not one of their gifts. And none of these approaches addressed the issue of how Christians' faith should affect the *way* they worked.

The start-up tech world, especially in the 1990s, was rather full of itself. Entrepreneurs and engineers were viewed as gods in our culture, and technology was the answer to all the world's problems. My employees had more evangelical fervor about the vision (and technologies) of the company than the people in any church I'd ever seen. And the hope of an IPO was far more tangible and motivational than the ethereal imaginings of heaven as portrayed by the Christian world. Much of the time I worked with really good people—mature, admirable people of character who worked hard to contribute significantly to the world and who didn't seem to need church or the Jesus of the Bible to do it. I learned great lessons about joy at work, patience and hope, teamwork and truth telling, from people who didn't share my faith. My staff who went away for a meditation weekend seemed to come back more refreshed than those who worshipped together on Sunday at a Christian evangelical church. I started to see my work more as a crucible where God was pounding and grinding and refining me, rather than as a place where I was actively and effectively serving him.

I believed in the truth of the gospel—that God created all things and created man in his image and then sent his Son to redeem all things that had been broken. And I believed God had a purpose for me as a worker and leader, along with many other people who could make a positive difference in the world. But in the competitive, win-at-all-costs workplace where I had to manage and lead, I had no idea how to live out God's plan.

Outside of Redeemer, the churches I found didn't seem to offer much guidance on how I should do this. Most pastors were more concerned about helping us serve inside the church than about discipling and equipping us to serve in the world. In the boom times of Silicon Valley in the late 1990s, many congregations seemed oblivious to any brokenness in the world or in themselves. Many who cared deeply about the poor didn't think about how the systems, structures, and cultures of our industries might actually be contributing to the fractures in our culture. Living out my faith in my work seemed relegated to small symbolic gestures, to self-righteous abstinence from certain behaviors, and to political alignments on the top cultural and legal issues of the day.

The last company I led provided a remarkable leadership experience. I took over from the founder, who had wooed most of the staff and early customers to a wonderful vision of product innovation and IPO riches. In early 2000 we were being fought over by investment banks that courted us with potential IPO valuations of 200 to 350 million dollars. We didn't yet have products, but several were in beta mode with early adopters. My job was to win the trust of the staff, investors, and customers, while rolling out products that delivered on our promises and raising new money to get us to break even. There was pressure every day to make progress in all these areas. In the process I thought desperately about how the gospel should enter into all this. Here are some of the observations I made at the time:

- The gospel assures me that God cares about everything I do and will listen to my prayers. He may not answer them the way I want, but if he doesn't it is because he knows things I do not. My degree of success or failure is part of his good plan for me. God is my source of strength and perseverance.
- The gospel reminds us that God cares about the products we make, the companies we work for, and the customers we serve. He not only loves us, but also loves the world and wants us to serve it well. My work is a critical way in which God is caring for human beings and renewing his world. God gives us our vision and our hope.
- The gospel is good news. In the words of pastor and counselor Jack Miller, "Cheer up: You're a worse sinner

than you ever dared imagine, and you're more loved than you ever dared hope."[1] In other words, I will continually err and sin, and yet God will prevail in my life through his goodness and grace.

- The gospel gives meaning to our work as leaders. We're supposed to treat all people and their work with dignity. We're to create an environment in which people can flourish and use their God-given gifts to contribute to society. We're to embody grace, truth, hope, and love in the organizations we create.
- We're to express our relationship with God and his grace to us in the way we speak, work, and lead, not as perfect exemplars but as pointers to Christ.

After eighteen months of relentless work, the company failed. We were part of the Internet bubble, and when it burst, it took us with it. While we got our product to market on schedule, we couldn't raise the additional money we needed after venture capital dried up. We retained bankers to shop for a buyer that would enable us to at least keep the product going, keep some of the staff working, and provide some return to our investors. However, the fears in the market scared off the buyer we had been courting just days before signing the deal. I had to lay off a hundred people the next day and then sell off our intellectual property.

How could all this good, hard work go so wrong? My questions and protests to God were on a personal, company, and industry level. Why didn't God enable our success when he so clearly had "called" me to this job? I had tried to do right by our employees, and now they were out of work in a collapsed market.

I wondered if I had fed into this Internet "bubble and bust" with our company's own vision of skyrocketing revenues and valuations. What were my responsibilities to all our stakeholders, including the culture at large? The only Christian businesspeople I'd heard speak were those who gave God credit for their big successes; how was I to handle a failure? I wanted a gospel that had good news even for this.

An amazing thing happened when I announced that the next day would be our last day, although it took me some time to fully appreciate the full beauty and gift of it. The staff, entirely on their own, made a plan to come in the following day—for no pay—to celebrate one another and the work they had done. Though the celebration was bittersweet, they brought in musical instruments to play for one another or demonstrated the tai chi they taught in the evenings, and they laughed about fun times together. I was amazed. They were honoring a culture, an organization, in which they'd found some joy in their work and in their relationships with one another—despite the end result. Eventually I came to see that day as a glimpse of God at work, doing what God does: healing and renewing and redeeming.

I suppose it could be called poetic justice that the response to all my disillusionment about the lack of support from churches was that six months later, Redeemer Presbyterian Church invited me to move back to New York to help them start a ministry for people in the marketplace. After a decade of wrestling with God, pondering the transformational power of the gospel, and complaining about the lack of guidance and support from the church regarding work, I was being given a chance to help others better live out the hope and truth of the gospel in their vocational callings.

Foreword

This book captures some foundational ways of thinking about God, Jesus, the Holy Spirit; who we are in relation to that Trinity; and how all this affects the work we were created to do. How we work—in the context of our particular culture, time in history, vocation, and organization—is something we all need to be thinking through in our own communities. But the answers will all hang on this essential theology: the knowledge of who God is, his relation to man, his plan for the world, and how the good news (or gospel) of Christ turns our lives and the way we work upside down.

I'm grateful to Tim Keller for the way he's applied the gospel to our work lives over the course of his preaching and leading in the last twenty-five years. And I'm grateful that he's taken the time to put these foundations into print in this book, so that all of us can dig more deeply into how God is calling us to live faithfully as we work.

Katherine Leary Alsdorf
Executive Director, Redeemer's Center for Faith & Work

INTRODUCTION

The Importance of Recovering Vocation

Robert Bellah's landmark book, *Habits of the Heart,* helped many people name the thing that was (and still is) eating away at the cohesiveness of our culture—"expressive individualism." Elsewhere, Bellah argued that Americans had created a culture that elevated individual choice and expression to such a level that there was no longer any shared life, no commanding truths or values that tied us together. As Bellah wrote, ". . . we are moving to an ever greater validation of the sacredness of the individual person, [but] our capacity to imagine a social fabric that would hold individuals together is vanishing. . . . The sacredness of the individual is not balanced by any sense of the whole or concern for the common good."[2] But near the end of *Habits,* the author proposes one measure that would go a long way toward reweaving the unraveling culture:

> To make a real difference . . . [there would have to be] a reappropriation of the idea of vocation or calling, a return in a new way to the idea of work as a contribution to the good of all and not merely as a means to one's own advancement.[3]

That is a remarkable statement. If Bellah is right, one of the hopes for our unraveling society is the recovery of the idea that all human work is not merely a job but a *calling*. The Latin word *vocare*—to call—is at the root of our common word "vocation." Today the word often means simply a job, but that was not the original sense. A job is a vocation only if someone else calls you to do it and you do it for them rather than for yourself. And so our work can be a calling only if it is reimagined as a mission of service to something beyond merely our own interests. As we shall see, thinking of work mainly as a means of self-fulfillment and self-realization slowly crushes a person and—as Bellah and many others have pointed out—undermines society itself.

But if we are to "reappropriate" an older idea, we must look at that idea's origin. In this case, the source of the idea of work as vocation is the Christian Scriptures. And so, taking our cue from Bellah's challenge, in this book we will do what we can to help illuminate the transformative and revolutionary connection between Christian faith and the workplace. We'll be referring to this connection—and all the ideas and practices surrounding it—as the "integration of faith and work."

The Many "Streams" of Faith and Work

We are not alone in this attempt. Perhaps not since the Protestant Reformation has there been so much attention paid to the relationship of Christian faith to work as there is today. The number of books, scholarly projects, academic programs, and online discussions on this subject has grown exponentially in the past two decades. Nevertheless, Christians who are seeking practical guidance for their work are often poorly served by this growing movement. Some, like Katherine Alsdorf (see the Foreword), have been frustrated by the shallowness of the advice and examples. Others are bewildered by the diversity—some would say cacophony—of voices giving counsel on how to be a Christian at work.

We can think of the current "faith and work movement" as a river being fed by a number of streams from very different head-waters. Perhaps most of the energy and most of the groups seeking to help people integrate faith and work are those with an evangelical understanding of the Bible and the Christian faith, but there have been very significant contributions from other traditions and wings of the faith. The ecumenical movement has contributed an emphasis on Christians using their work to further social justice in the world. That helped us understand that faithful work demands the application of distinctly Christian ethics.[4] The small group movement of the twentieth century emphasized the need for believers to give one another nurture and support for the struggles and hardships of work. This showed us that faithful work requires inner spiritual renewal and heart transformation.[5] The revivalist impulse within evangelicalism has seen the workplace especially as a place to be a witness for Jesus Christ.[6] Faithful work indeed means some kind of public identification with Jesus, in such a way that a coworker might want to know more about him.

Many have also sought older sources for the integration of faith and work. The sixteenth-century Protestant Reformers, particularly Martin Luther and John Calvin, argued that all work, even so-called secular work, was as much a calling from God as the ministry of the monk or priest.[7] The headwaters of Lutheran theology put special stress on the dignity of all work, observing that God cared for, fed, clothed, sheltered, and supported the human race through our human labor. When we work, we are, as those in the Lutheran tradition often put it, the "fingers of God," the agents of his providential love for others. This understanding elevates the purpose of work from making a living to loving our neighbor and at the same time releases us from the crushing burden of working primarily to prove ourselves. Those in the Calvinist, or "Reformed," tradition, such as Abraham Kuyper, spoke of another aspect to the idea of work as God's calling. Work not only cares for creation, but also directs and structures it. In this Reformed view, the purpose of work is to create a culture that honors God and enables people to thrive. Yes, we must love our neighbor, but Christianity gives us very specific teachings about human nature and what makes human beings flourish. We must ensure that our work is done in line with these understandings. Faithful work, then, is to operate out of a Christian "worldview."[8]

All of these different traditions give somewhat different answers to the question of how we should go about the task of recapturing vocation. The streams are often confusing to Christians, for they are not perfectly complementary to one another. Lutheran theology tends to resist the Reformed idea of "worldview" and argues that Christians should not do their work in a very different way from non-Christians. Much of the mainline church does not feel the same urgency that evangelicals feel to evangelize, because it does not see classical Christianity as the only way to salvation. Many find the emphasis of worldview-oriented writers and organizations to be too cognitive, with too little emphasis on inner heart change. And even those people cannot agree on what inner transformation and spiritual growth actually look like. So if you are a Christian who is trying to be faithful in your work, you might find yourself trying to weigh sentiments as varied as these:

- The way to serve God at work is to further social justice in the world.

- The way to serve God at work is to be personally honest and evangelize your colleagues.

- The way to serve God at work is just to do skillful, excellent work.

- The way to serve God at work is to create beauty.

- The way to serve God at work is to work from a Christian motivation to glorify God, seeking to engage and influence culture to that end.

- The way to serve God at work is to work with a grateful, joyful, gospel-changed heart through all the ups and downs.

- The way to serve God at work is to do whatever gives you the greatest joy and passion.

- The way to serve God at work is to make as much money as you can, so that you can be as generous as you can.

To what extent are these sentiments complementary or actually opposed to one another? That is a difficult question, for there is at least a measure of biblical warrant for every one of them. And the difficulty lies not merely in the plethora of theological commitments and cultural factors involved, but also in how they operate in different ways depending on the field or type of work. Christian ethics, motives, identity, witness, and worldview shape our work in very different ways depending on the form of the work.

For example, suppose a Christian visual artist regularly shows concern for justice, conducts her career with honesty in all transactions, has support from others to help her navigate the ups and downs of life, lets others in her field know of her Christian faith, and understands her art to be an act of service to God and her neighbors rather than as a way to get self-worth and status. Is that all it means to integrate her faith with her work? In addition to these, does the Christian teaching about the nature of reality bear on what she depicts and how she depicts it through her art? Will it influence what stories she tells with her art? Will her art be influenced by her beliefs about sin and redemption and hope for the future? It seems that it must be. And so we discover that faithful work requires the will, the emotions, the soul, and the mind—as we think out and live out the implications of our beliefs on the canvas of our daily work.

On the other hand, what if you are a Christian pianist, or a shoemaker? How does a Christian worldview affect the type of shoe you make, or the way you play the *Moonlight Sonata*? The answer is not so clear.

Who will deliver us from all this complexity? Most people who have begun to read books or become involved in groups integrating faith and work have either (a) only partaken of one of the theological streams or (b) already been confused by reading or hearing contradictory teaching from different streams. There is a tendency for churches and organizations emphasizing faith and work to be somewhat unbalanced, emphasizing one or two of these story lines to the exclusion of the others. Yet simply combining all the emphases—and hoping they add up to something coherent—is not the solution.

We do not expect to resolve all these differences in this book. But we do hope to make things clearer. And we can begin by making two observations about the list of propositions above. First, if you revise each of the propositions by adding the word "main"—as in "the *main* way to serve God at work is . . ."—then the views do in fact contradict. You will have to choose one or two and discard the rest. In fact, most people who hold forth on issues of faith and work do exactly this, either tacitly or explicitly. But if you keep the propositions the way they are, claiming that each is *a* way to serve God through work, then the different statements are ultimately complementary. Second, as we have already noted, these factors can assume very different forms and levels of importance depending on your particular vocation, culture, and historical moment. When we keep these two principles in mind, we can move forward looking at the various streams, statements, and truths as a kind of tool kit to be used to build a model for the integration of faith and work in your field, time, and place.

Just as important as making these ideas clearer, we aim to make them more vivid, real, and practical. Our goal is to feed your imagination and stir your action with the richness of what the Christian faith says (directly and indirectly) about this inexhaustible subject. The Bible teems with wisdom, resources, and hope for anyone who is learning to work, looking for work, trying to work, or going to work. And when we say that the Christian Scriptures "give us hope" for work, we at once acknowledge both how deeply frustrating and difficult work can be and how profound the spiritual hope must be if we are going to face the challenge of pursuing vocation in this world. I know of no more provocative witness to this hope than the overlooked little story by J.R.R. Tolkien "Leaf by Niggle."

There Really Is a Tree

When J.R.R. Tolkien had been working on writing *The Lord of the Rings* for some time, he came to an impasse.[9] He had a vision of a tale of a sort that the world had never seen. As a leading scholar in Old English and other ancient Northern European languages, he knew that most ancient British myths about the inhabitants of "Faerie"—elves, dwarves, giants, and sorcerers—had been lost (unlike the myths of the Greeks and Romans or even of the Scandinavians). He had always dreamed of re-creating and re-imagining what an ancient English mythology would look like. *The Lord of the Rings* was rooted in this lost world. The project required creating at least the rudiments of several imaginary languages and cultures as well as thousands of years of various national histories—all in order to give the narrative the necessary depth and realism that Tolkien believed was crucial for the tale to be compelling.

As he worked on the manuscript, he came to the place where the narrative had divided into a number of subplots. Major characters were traveling to various parts of his imaginary world, facing different perils, and experiencing several complicated chains of events. It was an enormous challenge to unfold all these subnarratives clearly and then give each a satisfactory resolution. Not only that, but World War II had begun, and though the fifty-year-old Tolkien was not called into the military, the shadow of war fell heavily on him. He had experienced firsthand the horror of World War I and had never forgotten it. Britain was now in a precarious position, with invasion imminent. Who knew if he'd survive the war even as a civilian?

He began to despair of ever completing the work of his life. It was not just a labor of a few years at that point. When he began *The Lord of the Rings*, he had already been working on the languages, histories, and stories behind the story for decades. The thought of not finishing it was "a dreadful and numbing thought."[10] There was in those days a tree in the road near Tolkien's house, and one day he arose to find that it had been lopped and mutilated by a neighbor. He began to think of his mythology as his "internal Tree" that might suffer the same fate. He had run out of "mental energy and invention."[11] One morning he woke up with a short story in his mind and wrote it down. When *The Dublin Review* called for a piece, he sent it in with the title "Leaf by Niggle." It was about a painter.

In the first lines of the story we are told two things about this painter. First, his name was Niggle. The *Oxford English Dictionary*, to which Tolkien was a contributor, defines "niggle" as "to work . . . in a fiddling or ineffective way . . . to spend time unnecessarily on petty details."[12] Niggle was of course Tolkien himself, who knew very well this was one of his own flaws. He was a perfectionist, always unhappy with what he had produced, often distracted from more important issues by fussing over less important details, prone to worry and procrastination. Niggle was the same.

We are also told that Niggle "had a long journey to make. He did not want to go, indeed the whole idea was distasteful to him; but he could not get out of it." Niggle continually put the journey off, but he knew it was inevitable. Tom Shippey, who also taught Old English literature at Oxford, explains that in Anglo-Saxon literature the "necessary long journey" was death.[13]

Niggle had one picture in particular that he was trying to paint. He had gotten in his mind the picture of a leaf, and then that of a whole tree. And then in his imagination, behind the tree "a country began to open out; and there were glimpses of a forest marching over the land, and of mountains tipped with snow." Niggle lost interest in all his other pictures, and in order to accommodate his vision, he laid out a canvas so large he needed a ladder. Niggle knew he had to die, but he told himself, "At any rate, I shall get this one picture done, my real picture, before I have to go on that wretched journey."

So he worked on his canvas, "putting in a touch here, and rubbing out a patch there," but he never got much done. There were two reasons for this. First, it was because he was the "sort of painter who can paint leaves better than trees. He used to spend a long time on a single leaf, . . ." trying to get the shading and the sheen and the dewdrops on it just right. So no matter how hard he worked, very little actually showed up on the canvas itself. The second reason was his "kind heart." Niggle was constantly distracted by doing things his neighbors asked him to do for them. In particular, his neighbor Parish, who did not appreciate Niggle's painting at all, asked him to do many things for him.

One night when Niggle senses, rightly, that his time is almost up, Parish insists that he go out into the wet and cold to fetch a doctor for his sick wife. As a result he comes down with a chill and fever, and while working desperately on his unfinished picture, the Driver comes to take Niggle on the journey he has put off. When he realizes he must go, he bursts into tears. "'Oh, dear!' said poor Niggle, beginning to weep, 'And it's not even finished!'" Sometime after his death the people who acquired his house noticed that on his crumbling canvas his only "one beautiful leaf" had remained intact. It was put in the Town Museum, "and for a long while 'Leaf: by Niggle' hung there in a recess, and was noticed by a few eyes."

But the story does not end there. After death Niggle is put on a train toward the mountains of the heavenly afterlife. At one point on his trip he hears two Voices. One seems to be Justice, the severe voice, which says that Niggle wasted so much time and accomplished so little in life. But the other, gentler voice ("though it was not soft"), which seems to be Mercy, counters that Niggle has chosen to sacrifice for others, knowing what he was doing. As a reward, when Niggle gets to the outskirts of the heavenly country, something catches his eye. He runs to it—and there it is: "Before him stood the Tree, his Tree, finished; its leaves opening, its branches growing and bending in the wind that Niggle had so often felt or guessed, and yet had so often failed to catch. He gazed at the Tree, and slowly he lifted his arms and opened them wide. 'It is a gift!' he said."[14]

The world before death—his old country—had forgotten Niggle almost completely, and there his work had ended unfinished and helpful to only a very few. But in his new country, the permanently *real* world, he finds that his tree, in full detail and *finished*, was not just a fancy of his that had died with him. No, it was indeed part of the True Reality that would live and be enjoyed forever.[15]

I've recounted this story many times to people of various professions—particularly artists and other creatives—and regardless of their beliefs about God and the afterlife, they are often deeply moved. Tolkien had a very Christian understanding of art and, indeed, of all work.[16] He believed that God gives us talents and gifts so we can do for one another what he wants to do for us and through us. As a writer, for example, he could fill people's lives with meaning through the telling of stories that convey the nature of reality.[17] Niggle was assured that the tree he had "felt and guessed" was "a true part of creation"[18] and that even the small bit of it he had unveiled to people on earth had been a vision of the True. Tolkien was very comforted by his own story. It helped "exorcise some of Tolkien's fear, and to get him to work again," though it was also the friendship and loving prodding of C.S. Lewis that helped get him back to the writing.[19]

Artists and entrepreneurs can identify very readily with Niggle. They work from visions, often very big ones, of a world they can uniquely imagine. Few realize even a significant percentage of their vision, and even fewer claim to have come close. Those of us who tend to be overly perfectionistic and methodical, like Tolkien himself, can also identify strongly with the character of Niggle.

But really—everyone is Niggle. *Everyone* imagines accomplishing things, and everyone finds him- or herself largely incapable of producing them. Everyone wants to be successful rather than forgotten, and everyone wants to make a difference in life. But that is beyond the control of any of us. If this life is all there is, then everything will eventually burn up in the death of the sun and no one will even be around to remember anything that has ever happened. Everyone will be forgotten, nothing we do will make any difference, and all good endeavors, even the best, will come to naught.

Unless there is God. If the God of the Bible exists, and there is a True Reality beneath and behind this one, and this life is not the only life, then every good endeavor, even the simplest ones, pursued in response to God's calling, can matter forever. That is what the Christian faith promises. "In the Lord, your labor is not in vain," writes Paul in the first letter to the Corinthians, chapter 15, verse 58. He was speaking of Christian ministry, but Tolkien's story shows how this can ultimately be true of all work. Tolkien had readied himself, through Christian truth, for very modest accomplishment in the eyes of this world. (The irony is that he produced something so many people consider a work of genius that it is one of the bestselling books in the history of the world.)

What about you? Let's say that you go into city planning as a young person. Why? You are excited about cities, and you have a vision about how a real city ought to be. You are likely to be discouraged because throughout your life you probably will not get more than a leaf or a branch done. But there really is a New Jerusalem, a heavenly city, which will come down to earth like a bride dressed for her husband (Revelation 21–22).

Or let's say you are a lawyer, and you go into law because you have a vision for justice and a vision for a flourishing society ruled by equity and peace. In ten years you will be deeply disillusioned because you will find that as much as you are trying to work on important things, so much of what you do is minutiae. Once or twice in your life you may feel like you have finally "gotten a leaf out."

Whatever your work, you need to know this: There really is a tree. Whatever you are seeking in your work—the city of justice and peace, the world of brilliance and beauty, the story, the order, the healing—it is *there*. There is a God, there is a future healed world that he will bring about, and your work is showing it (in part) to others. Your work will be only partially successful, on your *best* days, in bringing that world about. But inevitably the whole tree that you seek—the beauty, harmony, justice, comfort, joy, and community—will come to fruition. If you know all this, you won't be despondent because you can get only a leaf or two out in this life. You will work with satisfaction and joy. You will not be puffed up by success or devastated by setbacks.

I just said, "*If* you know all this." In order to work in this way—to get the consolation and freedom that Tolkien received from his Christian faith for his work—you need to know the Bible's answers to three questions: Why do you *want* to work? (That is, why do we need to work in order to lead a fulfilled life?) Why is it so *hard* to work? (That is, why is it so often fruitless, pointless, and difficult?) How can we overcome the difficulties and find satisfaction in our work through the gospel? The rest of this book will seek to answer those three questions in its three sections, respectively.

PART ONE

God's Plan for Work

ONE

The Design of Work

Thus the heavens and the earth were finished, and all the host of them. And on the seventh day God finished his work that he had done, and he rested on the seventh day from all his work that he had done. So God blessed the seventh day and made it holy, because on it God rested from all his work that he had done in creation. . . . The Lord God took the man and put him in the garden of Eden to work it and keep it.

Genesis 2:1–3, 15 (ESV)

In the Beginning, There Was Work

The Bible begins talking about work as soon as it begins talking about anything—that is how important and basic it is. The author of the book of Genesis describes God's creation of the world as *work*.[20] In fact, he depicts the magnificent project of cosmos invention within a regular workweek of seven days.[21] And then he shows us human beings working in paradise. This view of work— connected with divine, orderly creation and human purpose—is distinct among the great faiths and belief systems of the world.

The creation narrative in the book of Genesis is unique among ancient accounts of origins. Many cultures had stories that depicted the beginning of the world and human history as the result of a struggle between warring cosmic forces. In the Babylonian creation story the *Enuma Elish*, the god Marduk overcomes the goddess Tiamat and forges the world out of her remains. In this and similar accounts, the visible universe was an uneasy balance of powers in tension with one another.[22] In the Bible, however, creation is not the result of a conflict, for God has no rivals. Indeed, all the powers and beings of heaven and earth are created by him and dependent on him.[23] Creation, then, is not the aftermath of a battle but the plan of a craftsman. God made the world not as a warrior digs a trench but as an artist makes a masterpiece.

The Greeks' account of creation includes the idea of successive "ages of mankind" beginning with a golden age. During this age human beings and gods lived on the earth together in harmony. This sounds at first vaguely like the story of the garden of Eden, but one dissimilarity is very telling. The poet Hesiod tells us that neither humans nor gods in the golden age had to do any work. In that original paradise the earth simply provided food in abundance.[24] The book of Genesis could not have been more different. Repeatedly the first chapters of the book of Genesis describe God at "work," using the Hebrew *mlkh*, the word for ordinary human work. As one scholar put it, it is wholly "unexpected that the extraordinary divine activity involved in creating heaven and earth should be so described."[25]

In the beginning, then, God worked. Work was not a necessary evil that came into the picture later, or something human beings were created to do but that was beneath the great God himself. No, God worked for the sheer joy of it. Work could not have a more exalted inauguration.

The Forms of God's Work

It is remarkable that in Chapter 1 of the book of Genesis, God not only works but finds delight in it. "God saw all that he had made, and it was very good . . . the heavens and the earth were completed in all their vast array" (Genesis 1:31; 2:1). God finds what he has done beautiful. He stands back, takes in "all that he has made," and says, in effect, "That's good!" Like all good and satisfying work, the worker sees himself in it. "The harmony and perfection of the completed heavens and earth express more adequately the character of their creator than any of the separate components can."[26]

The second chapter of Genesis goes on to show that God works not only to create but also to care for his creation. This is what theologians call the work of "providence." God creates human beings and then works for them as their Provider. He forms a man (Genesis 2:7), plants a garden for him and waters it (Genesis 2:6, 8), and fashions a wife for him (Genesis 2:21–22). The rest of the Bible tells us that God continues this work as Provider, caring for the world by watering and cultivating the ground (Psalm 104:10–22), giving food to all he has made, giving help to all who suffer, and caring for the needs of every living thing (Psalm 145:14–16).

Finally, we see God not only working, but commissioning workers to carry on his work. In Genesis chapter 1, verse 28 he tells human beings to "fill the earth and subdue it." The word "subdue" indicates that, though all God had made was good, it was still to a great degree undeveloped. God left creation with deep untapped potential for cultivation that people were to unlock through their labor.[27] In Genesis chapter 2, verse 15 (ESV) he puts human beings into the garden to "work it and keep it." The implication is that, while God works for us as our Provider, we also work for him. Indeed, he works *through* us. Psalm 127, verse 1—"Unless the Lord builds the house, the builders labor in vain"—indicates that God is building the house (providing for us) through the builders. As Martin Luther argued, Psalm 145 says that God feeds every living thing, meaning he is feeding us through the labor of farmers and others.[28]

The Goodness of Our Work

The book of Genesis leaves us with a striking truth—work was part of paradise. One biblical scholar summed it up: "It is perfectly clear that God's good plan always included human beings working, or, more specifically, living in the constant cycle of work and rest."[29] Again, the contrast with other religions and cultures could not be sharper. Work did not come in after a golden age of leisure. It was part of God's perfect design for human life, because we were made in God's image, and part of his glory and happiness is that he works, as does the Son of God, who said, "My Father is always at his work to this very day, and I too am working" (John 5:17).

The fact that God put work in paradise is startling to us because we so often think of work as a necessary evil or even punishment. Yet we do not see work brought into our human story after the fall of Adam, as part of the resulting brokenness and curse; it is part of the blessedness of the garden of God. Work is as much a basic human need as food, beauty, rest, friendship, prayer, and sexuality; it is not simply medicine but food for our soul. Without meaningful work we sense significant inner loss and emptiness. People who are cut off from work because of physical or other reasons quickly discover how much they need work to thrive emotionally, physically, and spiritually.

Our friends Jay and Barbara Belding, entrepreneurs in suburban Philadelphia, recognized this need even among developmentally disabled adults. While working as a special education teacher, Jay was disconcerted by the vocational prospects of his students once they completed school. Traditional vocational training and employment programs often had insufficient work and therefore extensive downtime with no wages. In 1977 Jay and Barbara established Associated Production Services, an enterprise providing quality training and employment for this population. Today the company trains 480 people who are engaged in a variety of labor-intensive packaging and assembly work for a number of consumer products companies at four facilities. Jay focuses on providing tools and systems that ensure quality and increase efficiencies and output; this helps create a culture of success for the company and the people they serve. The Beldings are thrilled and grateful to have found a practical, sustainable way to meet their employees' intrinsic need to be productive: "Our people want to participate in the 'work-a-day' world; to feel positive about themselves; and to help pay their own way." Their employees are finally able to respond fully to a vital aspect of their design as workers and creators.

Work is so foundational to our makeup, in fact, that it is one of the few things we can take in significant doses without harm.

Indeed, the Bible does not say we should work one day and rest six, or that work and rest should be balanced evenly—but directs us to the opposite ratio. Leisure and pleasure are great goods, but we can take only so much of them. If you ask people in nursing homes or hospitals how they are doing, you will often hear that their main regret is that they wish they had something to do, some way to be useful to others. They feel they have too much leisure and not enough work. The loss of work is deeply disturbing because we were designed for it. This realization injects a deeper and far more positive meaning into the common view that people work in order to survive. According to the Bible, we don't merely need the money from work to survive; we need the work itself to survive and live fully human lives.

The reasons for this are developed more fully in later chapters, but they include the fact that work is one of the ways we make ourselves useful to others, rather than just living a life for ourselves. Also, work is also one of the ways we discover who we are, because it is through work that we come to understand our distinct abilities and gifts, a major component in our identities.[30] So author Dorothy Sayers could write, "What is the Christian understanding of work?. . . [It] is that work is not, primarily, a thing one does to live, but the thing one lives to do. It is, or it should be, the full expression of the worker's faculties . . . the medium in which he offers himself to God."[31]

The Freedom of Our Work

To see work in our "DNA," our design, is part of what it means to grasp the distinct Christian understanding of freedom. Modern people like to see freedom as the complete absence of any constraints. But think of a fish. Because a fish absorbs oxygen from water, not air, it is free only if it is restricted to water. If a fish is "freed" from the river and put out on the grass to explore, its freedom to move and soon even to live is destroyed. The fish is not more free, but less free, if it cannot honor the reality of its nature. The same is true with airplanes and birds. If they violate the laws of aerodynamics, they will crash into the ground. But if they follow them, they will ascend and soar. The same is true in many areas of life: Freedom is not so much the absence of restrictions as finding the right ones, those that fit with the realities of our own nature and those of the world.[32]

So the commandments of God in the Bible are a means of liberation, because through them God calls us to be what he built us to be. Cars work well when you follow the owner's manual and honor the design of the car. If you fail to change the oil, no one will fine you or take you to jail; your car will simply break down because you violated its nature. You suffer a natural consequence. In the same way, human life works properly only when it is conducted in line with the "owner's manual," the commandments of God. If you disobey the commands, not only do you grieve and dishonor God, you are actually acting against your own nature as God designed you. When God speaks to disobedient Israel in Isaiah chapter 48, he says, "I am the Lord your God, who teaches you what is best for you, who directs you in the way you should go. If only you had paid attention to my commands, your peace would have been like a river, your well-being like the waves of the sea" (Isaiah 48:17–18).

And so it is with work, which (in rhythm with rest) is one of the Ten Commandments. "Six days you shall labor and do all your work" (Exodus 20:9). In the beginning God created us to work, and now he calls us and directs us unambiguously to live out that part of our design. This is not a burdensome command; it is an invitation to freedom.

The Limits of All Work

Nevertheless, it is meaningful that God himself rested after work (Genesis 2:2). Many people make the mistake of thinking that work is a curse and that something else (leisure, family, or even "spiritual" pursuits) is the only way to find meaning in life. The Bible, as we have seen and will see, exposes the lie of this idea. But it also keeps us from falling into the opposite mistake, namely, that work is the only important human activity and that rest is a necessary evil—something we do strictly to "recharge our batteries" in order to continue to work. We look to what we know about God to make this case. He did not need any restoration of his strength—and yet he rested on the seventh day (Genesis 2:1–3). As beings made in his image, then we can assume that rest, and the things you do as you rest, are good and life-giving in and of themselves. Work is not all there is to life. You will not have a meaningful life without work, but you cannot say that your work is *the* meaning of your life. If you make any work the purpose of your life—even if that work is church ministry—you create an idol that rivals God. Your relationship with God is the most important foundation for your life, and indeed it keeps all the other factors—work, friendships and family, leisure and pleasure—from becoming so important to you that they become addicting and distorted.

Josef Pieper, a twentieth-century German Catholic philosopher, wrote a famous essay called "Leisure, the Basis of Culture." Pieper argues that leisure is not the mere absence of work, but an attitude of mind or soul in which you are able to contemplate and enjoy things as they are in themselves, without regard to their value or their immediate utility. The work-obsessed mind—as in our Western culture—tends to look at everything in terms of efficiency, value, and speed. But there must also be an ability to enjoy the most simple and ordinary aspects of life, even ones that are not strictly useful, but just delightful. Surprisingly, even the reputedly dour Reformer John Calvin agrees. In his treatment of the Christian life, he warns against valuing things only for their utility:

> Did God create food only to provide for necessity [nutrition] and not also for delight and good cheer? So too the purpose of clothing apart from necessity [protection] was comeliness and decency. In grasses, trees, and fruits, apart from their various uses, there is beauty of appearance and pleasantness of fragrance. . . . Did he not, in short, render many things attractive to us, apart from their necessary use?[33]

In other words, we are to look at everything and say something like:

> All things bright and beautiful; all creatures great and small
> All things wise and wonderful—the Lord God made them all.[34]

Unless we regularly stop work and take time to worship (which Pieper considers one of the chief activities within "leisure") and simply contemplate and enjoy the world—including the fruit of our labor—we cannot truly experience meaning in our lives. Pieper writes:

> Leisure is the condition of considering things in a celebrating spirit. . . . Leisure lives on affirmation. It is not the same as the absence of activity. . . . It is rather like the stillness in the conversation of lovers, which is fed by their oneness. . . . And as it is written in the Scriptures, God saw, when "he rested from all the works that He had made" that everything was good, very good (Genesis 1:31), just so the leisure of man includes within itself a celebratory, approving, lingering gaze of the inner eye on the reality of creation.[35]

In short, work—and lots of it—is an indispensable component in a meaningful human life. It is a supreme gift from God and one of the main things that gives our lives purpose. But it must play its proper role, subservient to God. It must regularly give way not just to work stoppage for bodily repair but also to joyful reception of the world and of ordinary life.

This may seem obvious to us. We say, "Of course work is important, and of course it isn't the only thing in life." But it is crucial to grasp these truths well. For in a fallen world, work is frustrating and exhausting; one can easily jump to the conclusion that work is to be avoided or simply endured. And because our disordered hearts crave affirmation and validation, it is just as tempting to be thrust in the opposite direction—making life all about career accomplishment and very little else. In fact, overwork is often a grim attempt to get our lifetime's worth of work out of the way early, so we can put work behind us. These attitudes will only make work more stultifying and unsatisfying in the end.

When we think, "I hate work!" we should remember that, despite the fact that work can be a particularly potent reminder (and even amplifier) of the curse of sin on all things, it is not itself a curse. We were built for it and freed by it. But when we feel that our lives are completely absorbed by work, remember that we must also honor work's limits. There is no better starting point for a meaningful work life than a firm grasp of this balanced work and rest theology.

TWO

The Dignity of Work

Then God said, "Let us make mankind in our image, in our likeness, so that they may rule over the fish in the sea and the birds in the sky, over the livestock and all the wild animals, and over all the creatures that move along the ground."

So God created mankind in his own image, in the image of God he created them; male and female he created them.

Genesis 1:26–27

Work as a Demeaning Necessity

Ayn Rand is one of the most widely read twentieth-century philosophers on the subject of work. In her two most famous novels, she creates characters who push against the trends of socialism and collectivism. Howard Roark, the architect in *The Fountainhead*, stirs the soul with his passion for creating buildings that creatively use the resources of the natural environment, tastefully complement their natural surroundings, and efficiently serve the needs of their intended occupants. Rand portrays him as fully human, in comparison to other architects who do their work for money or prestige. In *Atlas Shrugged* we have a very different hero, John Galt, who leads a strike by the society's most productive people, who refuse to be exploited any longer. He hopes to demonstrate that a world in which persons are not free to create is doomed. To Rand, creative, productive work is essential to human dignity but is typically demeaned by bureaucracy and commonness. One of her characters in *Atlas Shrugged* states, "Whether it's a symphony or a coal mine, all work is an act of creating and comes from the same source: . . . the capacity to see, to connect and to make what had not been seen, connected and made before."[36]

Rand has glimpsed one of the core aspects of man's dignity, as we come to understand it from reading Genesis 1. Unfortunately, she also was one of the twentieth century's most vocal critics of Christianity, rejecting the God of the Bible who made man in his own image. Still, we see that work is a major component of human dignity—it resonates today even with the most secular thinkers. That was not always so.

The ancient Greeks, who also thought that the gods made human beings for work, saw this as no blessing. Work was demeaning. As Italian philosopher Adriano Tilgher put it, "To the Greeks, work was a curse and nothing else."[37] In fact, Aristotle said that unemployment—by which he meant the ability to live without having to work—was a primary qualification for a genuinely worthwhile life.[38] What led the Greeks to this view of work?

Plato in his dialogue *Phaedo* argues that being in the body distorts and hampers the soul in its quest for truth. In this life, the person who develops spiritual insight and purity must do so by ignoring the body as much as possible. Death is therefore a form of liberation and even a friend of the soul.[39] "The Greek philosophers largely thought of the gods as perfect minds—solitary, self-sufficient, uninvolved in the stuff of the world or the hubbub of human affairs. Human beings were to become like the gods by withdrawing from active life and devoting themselves to contemplation."[40] Contemplation helped you realize that the material world is temporary and even illusory, and that being overinvolved or emotionally attached to it pulls you down into a kind of animal existence of fear, anger, and anxiety. Instead, the way to true peace and happiness was to learn how to achieve a "non-attachment" to the things of this world. Epictetus taught his disciples that "the good life is a life stripped of both hopes and fears. In other words, a life reconciled to what is the case, a life which accepts the world as it is."[41] To be most human was to be the least involved, and the least invested, in the material world.

Work, then, was a barrier to the highest kind of life. Work made it impossible to rise above the earthbound humdrum of life into the realm of philosophy, the domain of the gods. The Greeks understood that life in the world required work, but they believed that not all work was created equal. Work that used the mind rather than the body was nobler, less beastly. The highest form of work was the most cognitive and the least manual. "The whole Greek social structure helped to support such an outlook, for it rested on the premise that slaves and [craftsmen] did the work, enabling the elite to devote themselves to the exercise of the mind in art, philosophy, and politics."[42] Aristotle very famously said in his *Politics* I.V.8 that some people are born to be slaves. He meant that some people are not as capable of higher rational thought and therefore should do the work that frees the more talented and brilliant to pursue a life of honor and culture.

Modern people bristle with outrage at such a statement, but while we do not today hold with the idea of literal slavery, the attitudes behind Aristotle's statement are alive and well. Christian philosopher Lee Hardy and many others have argued that this "Greek attitude toward work and its place in human life was largely preserved in both the thought and practice of the Christian church" through the centuries, and still holds a great deal of influence today in our culture.[43] What has come down to us is a set of pervasive ideas.

One is that work is a necessary evil. The only good work, in this view, is work that helps make us money so that we can support our families and pay others to do menial work. Second, we believe that lower-status or lower-paying work is an assault on our dignity. One result of this belief is that many people take jobs that they are not suited for at all, choosing to aim for careers that do not fit their gifts but promise higher wages and prestige. Western societies are increasingly divided between the highly remunerated "knowledge classes" and the more poorly remunerated "service sector," and most of us accept and perpetuate the value judgments that attach to these categories. Another result is that many people will choose to be unemployed rather than do work that they feel is beneath them, and most service and manual labor falls into this category. Often people who have made it into the knowledge classes show great disdain for the concierges, handymen, dry cleaners, cooks, gardeners, and others who hold service jobs.

Work as a Mark of Human Dignity

The biblical view of these matters is utterly different. Work of all kinds, whether with the hands or the mind, evidences our dignity as human beings—because it reflects the image of God the Creator in us. Biblical scholar Derek Kidner notices something profound in the creation of animals and human beings in Genesis chapter 1: Only man is set apart and given a job description, "an *office* (1:26b, 28b; 2:19; cf. Ps.8:4–8; James 3:7) . . ."[44] In other words, while the plants and animals are called to simply "teem" and "reproduce," only humans are explicitly given a job. They are called to "subdue" and "have dominion," or rule the earth.

We are given specific work to do because we are made in God's image. What does this mean? "The rulers of the ancient Near East set up images and statues of themselves in places where they exercised or claimed to exercise authority. The images represented the ruler himself as symbols of his presence and authority . . ."[45] The close connection of Genesis chapter 1, verse 26 with the mandate to "rule" shows that this act of ruling is a defining aspect of what it means to be made in God's image. We are called to stand in for God here in the world, exercising stewardship over the rest of creation in his place as his vice-regents. We share in doing the things that God has done in creation—bringing order out of chaos, creatively building a civilization out of the material of physical and human nature, caring for all that God has made. This is a major part of what we were created to be.

While the Greek thinkers saw ordinary work, especially manual labor, as relegating human beings to the animal level, the Bible sees all work as distinguishing human beings from animals and elevating them to a place of dignity. Old Testament scholar

Victor Hamilton notes that in surrounding cultures such as Egypt and Mesopotamia, the king or others of royal blood might be called the "image of God"; but, he notes, that rarefied term "was not applied to the canal digger or to the mason who worked on the ziggurat. . . . [But Genesis chapter 1 uses] royal language to describe simply 'man.' In God's eyes all of mankind is royal. The Bible democratizes the royalistic and exclusivistic concepts of the nations that surrounded Israel."[46]

Work has dignity because it is something that God does and because we do it in God's place, as his representatives. We learn not only that work has dignity in itself, but also that all *kinds* of work have dignity. God's own work in Genesis 1 and 2 is "manual" labor, as he shapes us out of the dust of the earth, deliberately putting a spirit in a physical body, and as he plants a garden (Genesis 2:8). It is hard for us today to realize how revolutionary this idea has been in the history of human thinking. Minister and author Phillip Jensen puts it this way: "If God came into the world, what would he be like? For the ancient Greeks, he might have been a philosopher-king. The ancient Romans might have looked for a just and noble statesman. But how does the God of the Hebrews come into the world? As a carpenter."[47]

The current economic era has given us fresh impulses and new ways to stigmatize work such as farming and caring for children—jobs that supposedly are not "knowledge" jobs and therefore do not pay very well. But in Genesis we see God as a gardener, and in the New Testament we see him as a carpenter. No task is too small a vessel to hold the immense dignity of work given by God. Simple physical labor is God's work no less than the formulation of theological truth. Think of the supposedly menial work of housecleaning. Consider that if you do not do it—or hire someone else to do it—you will eventually get sick and die from the germs, viruses, and infections that will breed in your home. The material creation was made by God to be developed, cultivated, and cared for in an endless number of ways through human labor. But even the simplest of these ways is important. Without them all, human life cannot flourish.

Mike, a friend of Katherine's, is a doorman in New York City. He is one of fifteen doormen serving a large Manhattan co-op; his apartment building is home to about one hundred families. Now in his early sixties, Mike emigrated to the U.S. from Croatia as a young man and worked in many kinds of jobs, from the restaurant business to manual labor. He has been a doorman in the building for twenty years and is clearly distinctive in his attitude toward his work. To Mike it's far from just a job. He cares about the people in the building and takes pride in helping with loading, finding parking spaces, and welcoming guests. He sets the standard for keeping the lobby and front of the building clean and attractive.

When asked what makes him drop what he's doing to get to the curb in time to help unload a resident's car after a weekend away he responds, "That's my job" or "They needed help." Why does he remember the name of every child? "Because they live here." At one point, to the question, "But why do you work so hard at every part of this job?" he replied, "I don't know . . . it's just what I need to be able to look at myself in the mirror in the morning. I couldn't live with myself if I didn't try my best every day." He appears to work out of gratefulness for the job and for his life. He is glad to be in this country and for the opportunities it has given him.

Most of the people Mike serves are professionals or businesspeople who are probably glad not to be doormen. Some might even find the work of a doorman demeaning if they had to do it themselves. But Mike's attitude shows that he recognizes the inherent dignity of the work he is doing; and in this, he brings out its goodness and worth.

The Material World Matters

All work has dignity because it reflects God's image in us, and also because the material creation we are called to care for is good. The Greeks saw death as a friend, because it liberated us from the prison of physical life. The Bible sees death not as a friend, but as an enemy (1 Corinthians 15:26), because the created world is a brilliant and beautiful good (Genesis 1:31), destined to exist forever (Revelation 22:1–5). Indeed, the biblical doctrine of creation harmonizes with the doctrine of the incarnation (in which God takes upon himself a human body) and of the resurrection (in which God redeems not just the soul but the body) to show how deeply "pro-physical" Christianity is. For Christians, even our ultimate future is a physical one. Some views of reality see the spiritual as more real and true than the physical; other, more naturalistic views see the spiritual as illusory and the physical as the only thing real; but neither is true of the Bible.

We acknowledge that the world is good. It is not the temporary theater for our individual salvation stories, after which we go to live disembodied lives in a different dimension. According to the Bible, this world is the forerunner of the new heavens and new earth, which will be purified, restored, and enhanced at the "renewal of all things" (Matthew 19:28; Romans 8:19–25). No other religion envisions matter and spirit living together in integrity forever. And so birds flying and oceans roaring and people eating, walking, and loving are permanently good things.

As we have seen, this means that Christians cannot look down on labor involving more intimate contact with the material world. Caring for and cultivating this material world has worth, even if it means cutting the grass. This also means that "secular" work has no less dignity and nobility than the "sacred" work of ministry. We are both body and soul, and the biblical ideal of *shalom* includes both physical thriving as well as spiritual. "Food that nourishes, roofs that hold out the rain, shade that protects from the heat of the sun. . . . the satisfaction of the material needs and desires of men and women . . . when businesses produce material things that enhance the welfare of the community, they are engaged in work that matters to God."[48]

In Psalm 65, verses 9–10 and Psalm 104, verse 30 we find God cultivating the ground by watering it through rain showers, and, through his Holy Spirit, "renewing the face of the ground." However, in John 16, verses 8–11, the Holy Spirit is said to convict and convince people of sin and God's judgment—which is something a preacher does. So here we have God's Spirit both gardening and preaching the gospel. Both are God's work. How can we say one kind of work is high and noble and the other low and debasing?

We have an excellent foundation if we understand the goodness of creation and the dignity of work. We work in a wondrous world that is designed at least partly for our pleasure. The author of Genesis tells us we should experience awe as we stand before the richness of the creation, for it teems with life. God seems to delight in diversity and creativity. Other places in the Bible speak of God's creative activity as being motivated by the sheer delight of creating (see Proverbs 8:27–31). This, too, is part of God's plan for what our work should be about, and what it would still be about if we had not experienced the fall, which marred everything including our labor.

We were built for work and the dignity it gives us as human beings, regardless of its status or pay. The practical implications of this principle are far-reaching. We have the freedom to seek work that suits our gifts and passions. We can be open to greater opportunities for work when the economy is weak and jobs are less plentiful. We no longer have any basis for condescension or superiority; nor is there any basis for envy or feelings of infidelity. And every Christian should be able to identify, with conviction and satisfaction, the ways in which his or her work participates with God in his creativity and cultivation. To help us do that, we turn to the biblical understanding of culture.

THREE

Work as Cultivation

God blessed them and said to them, "Be fruitful and increase in number; fill the earth and subdue it. Rule over the fish in the sea and the birds in the sky and over every living creature that moves on the ground."

Genesis 1:28

Now the Lord God had planted a garden in the east, in Eden; and there he put the man he had formed. The Lord God made all kinds of trees grow out of the ground—trees that were pleasing to the eye and good for food. . . . The Lord God took the man and put him in the Garden of Eden to work it and take care of it. And the Lord God commanded the man, "You are free to eat from any tree in the garden; but you must not eat from the tree of the knowledge of good and evil, for when you eat from it you will certainly die." The Lord God said, "It is not good for the man to be alone. I will make a helper suitable for him." Now the Lord God had formed out of the ground all the wild animals and all the birds in the sky. He brought them to the man to see what he would name them; and whatever the man called each living creature, that was its name. So the man gave names to all the livestock, the birds in the sky and all the wild animals. But for Adam no suitable helper was found. So the Lord God caused the man to fall into a deep sleep; and while he was sleeping, he took one of the man's ribs and then closed up the place with flesh. Then the Lord God made a woman from the rib he had taken out of the man, and he brought her to the man.

Genesis 2:8–9, 15–22

Filling and Subduing the Earth

Work is our design and our dignity; it is also a way to serve God through creativity, particularly in the creation of culture.

God put human beings into a garden. Hebrew scholar Derek Kidner argues that work was prominent among the full range of delights there: "The earthly paradise . . . is a model of parental care. The fledgling is sheltered but not smothered: on all sides discoveries and encounters await him to draw out his powers of discernment and choice, and there is ample nourishment for his aesthetic, physical and spiritual appetites; further, there is a man's work before him for body and mind (v. 15, 19)."[49] For our spiritual growth there was a divine Word to obey (verses 16–17). For our cultural and creative development there was the physical work of the tending of the garden (verse 15) and the mental stretching and understanding involved in the naming of the animals (verse 19). Finally, in the creation of Eve and of marriage, there was the provision for growing the human race into a full society (verses 19–24). All these endeavors were given as an elaboration on the overarching job description of Genesis 1, verse 28—to "fill the earth and subdue it." This command has been called the "cultural mandate." What does it mean?

First, we are called to "fill the earth"—to increase in number. While God usually says of plants and animals "let them" multiply (verses 11, 20a, 20b, 22, and 24), human beings are not only given a command to do so actively (verse 28a) but then receive a detailed job description (verses 28b–29). In other words, only humans are given multiplication as a task to fulfill with intention. But why would this be a job—isn't it just a natural process? Not exactly. Human beings "filling the earth" means something far than plants and animals filling the earth. It means civilization, not just procreation. We get the sense that God does not want merely more individuals of the human *species*; he also wants the world to be filled with a human *society*. He could have just spoken the word and created millions of people in thousands of human settlements, but he didn't. He made it our job to develop and build this society.

Second, we are called to "rule" the rest of creation and even to "subdue" it. What does that mean? The word "subdue" might be read to imply that the forces of nature were adversarial and needed to be conquered in some way. Some have complained that this text gives human beings a license to exploit nature. But that is not what it is talking about.[50] Remember that this mandate is given before the fall, before nature becomes subject to decay (Romans 8:17–27) and brings up thorns along with fruit (Genesis 3:17–19). There is still a primeval harmony within creation that no longer exists in the same way after the fall. So there is no violent intent to "subduing" the earth. Instead, "ruling" the world as God's image bearers should be seen as stewardship or trusteeship. God owns the world, but he has put it under our care to cultivate it. It is definitely not a mandate to treat the world and its resources as if they are ours to use, exploit, and discard as we wish.

Nevertheless, the word translated as "subdue" is a strong word that means real assertion of will. That is God's stance toward creation; when he first creates the material world, he does not have it spring into being all ready-made. Rather, it is "formless" and "empty" (1:2). God then addresses these conditions progressively during Genesis 1—through his work. He gives the world form. Where it is unshaped and undifferentiated, he distinguishes and elaborates. He takes the general and separates it into particulars, for example, "separating" sky from sea (1:7) and light from darkness (1:4). We even see this love of diversity in God's creation of Eve. God could easily have created humanity in only one form but instead created us in two genders, different and complementary, yet equal. The creation of Adam and Eve as gendered beings leads to biological procreation, another way in which we are, as beings in his image, carrying on the work he began at the beginning. And where things are empty, God fills them. On the first three days he creates realms (heavens, sky and waters, earth), and on the second three days he fills each realm with inhabitants (sun, moon and stars, birds and fish, animals and humans).

So the word "subdue" indicates that even in its original, unfallen form, God made the world to need work. He made it such that even *he* had to work for it to become what he designed it to be, to bring forth all its riches and potential. It is no coincidence that in Genesis 1, verse 28 God tells us to follow him in doing the same things that he has been doing—filling and subduing.

Culture Making with God

Philosopher Al Wolters writes:

> The earth had been completely unformed and empty;
> in the six-day process of development God had formed
> it and filled it—but not completely. People must now
> carry on the work of development: by being fruitful
> they fill it even more; by subduing it they must form it
> even more . . . as God's representatives, [we] carry on
> where God left off. But this is now to be a *human* de-
> velopment of the earth. The human race will fill the
> earth with its own kind, and it will form the earth for
> its own kind. From now on the development of the
> created earth will be *societal* and *cultural* in nature.[51]

If we are to be God's image-bearers with regard to creation,
then we will carry on his pattern of work. His world is not hos-
tile, so that it needs to be beaten down like an enemy. Rather, its
potential is undeveloped, so it needs to be cultivated like a garden. So we are not to relate to the world as park rangers, whose
job is not to change their space, but to preserve things as they
are. Nor are we to "pave over the garden" of the created world
to make a parking lot. No, we are to be *gardeners* who take an
active stance toward their charge. They do not leave the land as
it is. They rearrange it in order to make it most fruitful, to draw
the potentialities for growth and development out of the soil.
They dig up the ground and rearrange it with a goal in mind: to
rearrange the raw material of the garden so that it produces food,
flowers, and beauty. And that is the pattern for all work. It is

creative and assertive. It is rearranging the raw material of God's creation in such a way that it helps the world in general, and people in particular, thrive and flourish.

This pattern is found in all kinds of work. Farming takes the physical material of soil and seed and produces food. Music takes the physics of sound and rearranges it into something beautiful and thrilling that brings meaning to life. When we take fabric and make a piece of clothing, when we push a broom and clean up a room, when we use technology to harness the forces of electricity, when we take an unformed, naïve human mind and teach it a subject, when we teach a couple how to resolve their relational disputes, when we take simple materials and turn them into a poignant work of art—we are continuing God's work of forming, filling, and subduing. Whenever we bring order out of chaos, whenever we draw out creative potential, whenever we elaborate and "unfold" creation beyond where it was when we found it, we are following God's pattern of creative cultural development. In fact, our word "culture" comes from this idea of cultivation. Just as he subdued the earth in his work of creation, so he calls us now to labor as his representatives in a continuation and extension of that work of subduing.

At Redeemer we try to encourage our entrepreneurs—those who seek to create value out of the resources at their disposal to develop something new and innovative. One of those is James Tufenkian, who spoke at our annual forum for entrepreneurs in 2008. After developing several other businesses, James started making and distributing artisanal jams in 2005. He had been working in Armenia and was frustrated by the poverty and waste in that country. Vast areas of the country produced wonderful fruit, which were marketed and enjoyed in season, but large quantities were lost because of poor shipping and storage. He and a partner decided to launch a fruit preserve business and turn a seasonal rural business into a year-round venture. Harvest Song fruit preserves now win international awards for excellence and are sold around the world, because of the climate in which they're grown and the method through which they're preserved. According to James, one of his lifelong and faith-derived values is "making beautiful things of enduring value."[52] In fact, after studying God's work of forming and filling the earth and then looking back on it and saying "It was good," James had an epiphany. With delight he exclaimed, "God doesn't make junk. I don't make junk!" A biblical understanding of work energizes our desire to create value from the resources available to us. Recognizing the God who supplies our resources, and who gives us the privilege of joining in as cocultivators, helps us enter into our work with a relentless spirit of creativity.

Mark Noll writes in *The Scandal of the Evangelical Mind*,

> Who, after all, made the world of nature, and then made possible the development of sciences through which we find out more about nature? Who formed the universe of human interactions, and so provided the raw material for politics, economics, sociology, and history? Who is the source of harmony, form, and narrative pattern, and so lies behind all artistic and literary possibilities? Who created the human mind in such a way that it could grasp the endless realities of nature, of human interactions, of beauty, and so make possible the theories of such matters by philosophers and psychologists? Who moment by moment sustains the nat-

ural world, the world of human interactions, and the harmonies of existence? Who maintains moment by moment the connections between what is in our minds and what is in the world beyond our minds? The answer in every case is the same—God did it. And God does it.[53]

The naming of the animals in chapter 2, verses 19–20 is an invitation to enter into his creativity. Why didn't God just name the animals himself? After all, in Genesis 1, God names things, "calling" the light "Day" and the darkness "Night"—so he was clearly capable of naming the animals as well. Yet he invites us to continue his work of developing creation, to develop all the capacities of human and physical nature to build a civilization that glorifies him. Through our work we bring order out of chaos, create new entities, exploit the patterns of creation, and interweave the human community. So whether splicing a gene or doing brain surgery or collecting the rubbish or painting a picture, our work further develops, maintains, or repairs the fabric of the world. In this way, we connect our work to God's work.

All Work Is Culture Making

Fuller Seminary president Richard Mouw once addressed a number of bankers in New York City. He pointed them to Genesis and showed that God was a creator/investor who made the world as a home for all kinds of creativity. Mouw urged his audience to think of God as an investment banker. He leveraged his resources to create a whole world of new life. In the same way, what if you see a human need not being met, you see a talent or resource that can meet that need, and you then invest your resources—at your risk and cost—so that the need is met and the result is new jobs, new products, and better quality of life? What you are doing, Mouw concluded, is actually God-like.

After the address, many in the audience said, "Could you talk to my minister about this? He thinks that all I care about is making money." Indeed, not all business initiatives serve the common good.[54] But so many ministers assume that investors and entrepreneurs are solely out to make money without regard for advancing the common good. If ministers don't yet see business as a way of making culture and of cultivating creation, they will fail to support, appreciate, and properly lead many members of their congregation.

This aspect of the biblical understanding of work gives vision and meaning not only to ambitious endeavors, but even to the most commonplace ones; for it is equally necessary to cultivate creation in everyday ways. In his seminal and accessible book *Culture-Making: Recovering Our Creative Calling*, Andy Crouch reminds us that our work is important on any scale, whether grand or modest. Andy describes the impact made by his wife, Catherine, a professor of physics:

> In her work as a professor of physics, Catherine can do much to shape the culture of her courses and her research lab. In the somewhat sterile and technological environment of a laboratory, she can play classical music to create an atmosphere of creativity and beauty. She can shape the way her students respond to exciting and disappointing results, and can model both hard work and good rest rather than frantic work and fitful

procrastination. By bringing her children with her to work occasionally she can create a culture where family is not an interruption from work, and where research and teaching are natural parts of a mother's life; by inviting her students into our home she can show that she values them as persons, not just as units of research productivity. At the small scale of her laboratory and classroom, she has real ability to reshape the world.[55]

No everyday work lacks the dignity of being patterned after God's own work, yet no business megadeal or public policy initiative is so lofty that it can transcend God's patterns and limitations for work. What's more God has not left us alone to discover how or why we are to cultivate his creation; instead, he gives us a clear purpose for our work and faithfully calls us into it.

FOUR

Work as Service

Nevertheless, each person should live as a believer in whatever situation the Lord has assigned to them, just as God has called them. This is the rule I lay down in all the churches.

1 Corinthians 7:17

Called and Assigned

Mike Ullman, former CEO of JCPenney, tells of a conversation he had with Starbucks founder Howard Schultz when he was first offered the JCPenney position. Mike had retired from a long and successful career in retail management a few years before and was reluctant to get back into the business. But Schultz said to Ullman, "This opportunity is made for you. They need to put service back into the mission of that company, and you're the guy to do it." He didn't need the money or the recognition, but he agreed to take the role because he saw an opportunity to reorient twenty-five thousand retail employees to seeing that their work matters and that serving their customers is an honorable career. In short, he believed that God called him to a particular position of service.

We have been looking at the book of Genesis to understand the design, dignity, and pattern of work, but it is in the New Testament and particularly in the writings of Paul that we gain more insight into how God provides *purpose* for our work by calling us to serve the world.

Let's look at the biblical use of the term often translated as "calling." In the letters of the New Testament the Greek word for "to call" (*kaleo*) usually describes God's summons to men and women into saving faith and union with his Son (Romans 8:30; 1 Corinthians 1:9). It is also a call to serve him by reaching the world with his message (1 Peter 2:9–10). God's calling has not only an individual aspect but also a communal one. It brings you into a relationship not only with him, but also with a body of believers (1 Corinthians 1:9; Ephesians 1:1–4; Colossians 3:15). Indeed, the very Greek word for church—*ekklesia*—literally means the "ones called out."

In 1 Corinthians chapter 7, Paul counsels readers that when they become Christians it is unnecessary to change what they are currently doing in life—their marital state, job, or social station—in order to live their lives before God in a way that pleases him. In verse 17, Paul directs, "Only let each person lead the life that the Lord has assigned to him, and to which God has called him. This is my rule in all the churches."[57]

Here Paul uses two religiously freighted words to describe ordinary work. Elsewhere, Paul has spoken of God *calling* people into a saving relationship with him, and *assigning* them spiritual gifts to do ministry and build up the Christian community (Romans 12:3 and 2 Corinthians 10:13). Paul uses these same two words here when he says that every Christian should remain in the work God has "*assigned* to him, and to which God has *called* him." Yet Paul is not referring in this case to church ministries, but to common social and economic tasks—"secular jobs," we might say—and naming them God's callings and assignments.[57] The implication is clear: Just as God equips Christians for building up the Body of Christ, so he also equips all people with talents and gifts for various kinds of work, for the purpose of building up the human community.[58] Biblical scholar Anthony Thiselton writes about this passage: "This Pauline concept of call and service varies greatly from that of secular modernity, which gives a privileged place to 'autonomy,' and from that of secular postmodernity, which gives privilege to self-fulfillment and to power interests. . . . [It] gives this section [of Paul's writing] fresh relevance to the present."[59]

Thiselton's insight recalls the quote by Robert Bellah cited in our introduction. Bellah called us to recover the idea that work is a "vocation" or calling, "a contribution to the good of all and not merely . . . a means to one's own advancement," to one's self-fulfillment and power.[60] Remember that something can be a vocation or calling only if some other party calls you to do it, and you do it for their sake rather than for your own. Our daily work can be a calling only if it is reconceived as God's assignment to serve others. And that is exactly how the Bible teaches us to view work.

At our church we have many high-achieving young people who are recruited out of college or business school to work in the financial services industry. Lured by the recruiting process, signing bonuses, and compensation packages that far exceed those of other professions or industries, many of these young people barely consider other vocational alternatives. For decades these jobs have offered status and financial security beyond compare. In the face of this kind of opportunity, how is a committed Christian supposed to think objectively about his or her "calling"?

Certainly some do sense that their job in financial sales, trading, private equity, public finance, or a related area is a way for them to offer their unique capabilities in service to God and others. Some, however, after a few years on Wall Street, determine that their strengths and passions are more suited to another vocation. Jill Lamar, for example, worked several years at Merrill Lynch before deciding she needed to make a change. A lover of books and a good writer herself, she decided to switch to publishing, starting again at the very bottom in pay and position. She wrestled with the fact that the opportunity to make a lot of money didn't necessarily mean that banking was the vocation she should continue to pursue. She tried to think about how she could best use her gifts and passion to serve instead. Her decision created quite a flurry, even in the church!

Christians should be aware of this revolutionary understanding of the purpose of their work in the world. We are not to choose jobs and conduct our work to fulfill ourselves and accrue power, for being called by God to do something is empowering enough. We are to see work as a way of service to God and our neighbor, and so we should both choose and conduct our work in accordance with that purpose. The question regarding our choice of work is no longer "What will make me the most money and give me the most status?" The question must now be "How, with my existing abilities and opportunities, can I be of greatest service to other people, knowing what I do of God's will and of human need?"

Jill took this last question very seriously. In her subsequent years in publishing, she found that she was good at editing and at discovering new writers. She grew in her passion for giving the world good stories to read. Sometimes the stories reflected her biblical way of thinking about the world, but sometimes they did not. She was looking for excellence. Eventually she directed a wonderful program for Barnes & Noble called Discover Great New Writers. Through this initiative she was able to give worthy new authors a chance to find a broader audience of readers.

Notice something counterintuitive about the two questions on the previous page: It is the latter that will lead us to a more sustainable motivation for discipline and excellence at work. If the point of work is to serve and exalt ourselves, then our work inevitably becomes less about the work and more about us. Our aggressiveness will eventually become abuse, our drive will become burnout, and our self-sufficiency will become self-loathing. But if the purpose of work is to serve and exalt something *beyond* ourselves, then we actually have a better reason to deploy our talent, ambition, and entrepreneurial vigor—and we are more likely to be successful in the long run, even by the world's definition.

Vocation and the "Masks of God"

No one took hold of the teaching of the first book of Corinthians, chapter 7 more powerfully than Martin Luther. Luther translated the word "calling" in these verses as *Beruf* in German, the word for "occupation," and mounted a polemic against the view of vocation prevalent in the medieval church.[61] The church at that time understood itself as the entirety of God's kingdom on earth,[62] and therefore only work in and for the church could qualify as God's work. This meant that the only way to be called by God into service was as a monk, priest, or nun. They were called "the spiritual estate," everyone else's work was worldly, and secular labor was seen as akin to the demeaning necessity that the Greeks saw in manual labor.[63] Luther attacked this idea forcefully in his treatise *To the Christian Nobility of the German Nation*:

> It is pure invention [fiction] that Pope, bishops, priests, and monks are called the "spiritual estate" while princes, lords, artisans, and farmers are called the "temporal estate." This is indeed a piece of deceit and hypocrisy. Yet no one need be intimidated by it, and that for this reason: *all Christians are truly of the spiritual estate,* and there is no difference among them except that of office. . . . We are all consecrated priests by baptism, as St. Peter says: "You are a royal priesthood and a priestly realm" (1 Pet. 2:9). The Apocalypse says: "Thou hast made us to be kings and priests by thy blood" (Rev. 5:9–10).[64]

Luther is arguing here that God calls every Christian equally to their work. In his exposition of Psalm 147, Luther lays out his basic idea of vocation, explaining why this is so. He looks at verse 13, which assures a city that "God strengthens the bars of your gates."[65] Luther asks how God can strengthen the bars—provide for the security and safety—of a city. He answers, "By the word 'bars' we must understand not only the iron bar that a smith can make, but . . . everything else that helps to protect us, such as good government, good city ordinances, good order . . . and wise rulers. . . . this is a gift of God."[66] How does God give a city security? Isn't it through lawmakers, police officers, and those working in government and politics? So God cares for our civic needs through the work of others, whom he calls to that work.

In Luther's Large Catechism, when he addresses the petition in the Lord's Prayer asking God to give us our "daily bread," Luther says that "when you pray for 'daily bread' you are praying for everything that contributes to your having and enjoying your daily bread. . . . You must open up and expand your thinking, so that it reaches not only as far as the flour bin and baking oven but also out over the broad fields, the farmlands, and the entire country that produces, processes, and conveys to us our daily bread and all kinds of nourishment."[67] So how does God "feed every living thing" (Psalm 145:16) today? Isn't it through the farmer, the baker, the retailer, the website programmer, the truck driver, and all who contribute to bring us food? Luther writes: "God could easily give you grain and fruit without your plowing and planting, but he does not want to do so."[68]

Then he gives an analogy to show us why God works this way. Parents want to give their children everything they need, but they also want them to become diligent, conscientious, and responsible people. So they give their children chores. They could obviously do the chores better themselves, but that would not help their children grow in maturity. So parents give their children what they need—character—through the diligence required for the chores they assign them. Luther concludes that God works through our work for the same reason:

> What else is all our work to God—whether in the fields, in the garden, in the city, in the house, in war, or in government—but just such a child's performance, by which He wants to give His gifts in the

fields, at home, and everywhere else? These are the masks of God, behind which He wants to remain concealed and do all things.[69]

In his exposition of Psalm 147, verse 14, Luther goes on to ask, How does God "make peace in your borders?" His answer is, through good neighbors, who practice honesty and integrity in their daily interactions and who participate in civic life.[70] He even sees marital sexual relations as part of this pattern. God could have given us children directly. "He could give children without using men and women. But He does not want to do this. Instead, He joins man and woman so that it appears to be the work of man and woman but He does it under the cover of such masks."[71]

And so we see what Luther means by God's vocation. Not only are the most modest jobs—like plowing a field or digging a ditch—the "masks" through which God cares for us, but so are the most basic social roles and tasks, such as voting, participating in public institutions, and being a father or mother. These are all God's callings, all ways of doing God's work in the world, all ways through which God distributes his gifts to us. Even the humblest farm girl is fulfilling God's calling. As Luther preached, "God milks the cows through the vocation of the milk maids."[72]

Vocation and the Gospel

Luther contributed even more to our subject than this remarkable idea of all work as God's vocation. The doctrine of justification by faith alone—the foundational commitment of the Protestant Reformation—even more profoundly shapes the

Christian understanding of work. The older medieval view (of secular work as unimportant and religious work as exalted) was partially rooted in a misunderstanding regarding salvation itself. "In Luther's day," writes Lee Hardy, "it was generally held that the monks, by taking the monastic vows and submitting to the rigors of the cloistered life, could actually merit special divine favor and thereby make eternal salvation secure."[73] Luther realized, however, that all his exemplary religious observances and ministry did not free him from the reality that his life fell short of the righteousness God required. Then he made his famous discovery in Scripture that justification was by grace through faith in Christ apart from any good works of his own. He had been wrestling with the phrase "the righteousness of God" because "though I lived as a monk without reproach, I felt that I was a sinner before God with an extremely disturbed conscience. I could not believe that he was placated by my satisfaction [religious work]. . . . Thus I raged with a fierce and troubled conscience. . . ." He began to meditate on Romans 1, verses 16–17, where Paul says that salvation and the righteousness of God "is by faith." "Then," Luther wrote,

> I began to understand that the righteousness of God is that by which the righteous live by a gift of God, namely by faith. . . . Here I felt that I was altogether born again and had entered paradise itself through open gates. There a totally other face of the entire Scripture showed itself to me.[74]

As he observes in that last sentence, when he grasped that salvation was by grace rather than through any effort of his own, it made him rethink his whole understanding of Scripture, including his view of the meaning of work. Luther found two implications in particular. First, if religious works were crucial to achieving a good standing with God, then there would always be a fundamental difference between those in church ministry and everyone else. But if religious work did absolutely nothing to earn favor with God, it could no longer be seen as superior to other forms of labor.

The gospel of salvation through sheer grace holds a second implication for work. While ancient monks may have sought salvation through religious works, many modern people seek a kind of salvation—self-esteem and self-worth—from career success. This leads us to seek only high-paying, high-status jobs, and to "worship" them in perverse ways. But the gospel frees us from the relentless pressure of having to prove ourselves and secure our identity through work, for we are already proven and secure. It also frees us from a condescending attitude toward less sophisticated labor and from envy over more exalted work. All work now becomes a way to love the God who saved us freely; and by extension, a way to love our neighbor.

So Luther could write about believers: "Even their seemingly secular works are a worship of God and an obedience well pleasing to God."[75] He also said, "Why should I not therefore freely, joyfully, with all my heart, and with an eager will . . . give myself as a Christ to my neighbor, just as Christ offered himself to me . . . since through faith I have an abundance of all good things in Christ?"[76] Since we already have in Christ the things other people work for—salvation, self-worth, a good conscience, and peace—now we may work simply to love God and our neighbors. It is a sacrifice of joy, a limitation that offers freedom.

This means, ironically, that Christians who understand biblical doctrine ought to be the ones who appreciate the work of non-Christians the most. We know we are saved by grace alone, and therefore we are *not* better fathers or mothers, better artists and businesspersons, than those who do not believe as we do. Our gospel-trained eyes can see the world ablaze with the glory of God's work through the people he has created and called—in everything from the simplest actions, such as milking a cow, to the most brilliant artistic or historic achievements.

Work as an Act of Love

This revolutionary way of looking at work gives all work a common and exalted purpose: to honor God by loving your neighbors and serving them through your work.

Author Dorothy Sayers recounts how many British men and women stumbled upon something like this understanding of work during the dark days of World War II:

> The habit of thinking about work as something one does to make money is so ingrained in us that we can scarcely imagine what a revolutionary change it would be to think about it instead in terms of the work done [itself]. . . .[77] . . . I believe there is a Christian doctrine of work, very closely related to the doctrines of the creative energy of God and the divine image in man. . . . The essential [modern] heresy . . . being that work is not the expression of man's creative energy in the service of Society, but only something one does in order to obtain money and leisure.[78]

She goes on to explain what happens as a result: "Doctors practice medicine not primarily to relieve suffering, but to make a living—the cure of the patient is something that happens on the way. Lawyers accept briefs not because they have a passion for justice, but because the law is the profession which enables them to live." But during the war many people were drawn into the army and found a new, surprising sense of fulfillment in their work. "The reason why men often find themselves happy and satisfied in the army is that for the first time in their lives they found themselves doing something, not for the pay, which is miserable, but for the sake of getting the thing done."[79]

Sayers was talking about wartime Britain, in which every person knew that their work was contributing to the very survival of their nation. But author Lester DeKoster does an excellent job of showing how indispensible work is for human life in all times and places:

> Work is the form in which we make ourselves useful to others . . . in which others make themselves useful to us. We plant [with our work]; God gives the increase to unify the human race. . . .
>
> [Look at] the chair you are lounging in. . . . Could you have made it for yourself? . . . How [would you] get, say, the wood? Go and fell a tree? But only after first making the tools for that, and putting together some kind of vehicle to haul the wood, and constructing a mill to do the lumber and roads to drive on from place to place? In short, a lifetime or two to make one chair! . . . If we . . . worked not forty but one-hundred-forty hours per week we couldn't make ourselves from

scratch even a fraction of all the goods and services that we call our own. [Our] paycheck turns out to buy us the use of far more than we could possibly make for ourselves in the time it takes us to earn the check. . . . Work . . . yields far more in return upon our efforts than our particular jobs put in. . . .

Imagine that everyone quits working, right now! What happens? Civilized life quickly melts away. Food vanishes from the shelves, gas dries up at the pumps, streets are no longer patrolled, and fires burn themselves out. Communication and transportation services end, utilities go dead. Those who survive at all are soon huddled around campfires, sleeping in caves, clothed in raw animal hides. The difference between [a wilderness] and culture is simply, *work*.[80]

There may be no better way to love your neighbor, whether you are writing parking tickets, software, or books, than to simply do your work. But only skillful, competent work will do.

Work as a Ministry of Competence

One of the main ways that you love others in your work is through the "ministry of competence." If God's purpose for your job is that you serve the human community, then the way to serve God best is to do the job as well as it can be done. Dorothy Sayers writes,

The church's approach to an intelligent carpenter is usually confined to exhorting him to not be drunk and disorderly in his leisure hours and to come to church on Sundays. What the church should be telling him is this: that the very first demand that his religion makes upon him is that he should make good tables.[81]

Let me give a dramatic example of this. On February 24, 1989, United Airlines Flight 811 took off from Honolulu on its way to New Zealand. The 747 had climbed to twenty-two thousand feet when the forward cargo door of the jet blew open, tearing a huge hole in the side of the plane. Nine passengers were immediately sucked out of the plane to their deaths. The two right engines were damaged by flying debris and taken out of commission. The plane was one hundred miles from land. The captain, David Cronin, brought all of his wisdom and thirty-eight years of piloting experience to bear:

> To compensate for the lack of thrust from the two right engines, he struggled to hold the control column steady with his hands while using his feet to put pressure on the control floor rudder to stabilize the plane. His stickiest problem, however, was deciding how fast to fly. [He] slowed the plane as close to the stall speed as possible to keep the air rushing over the plane from further widening the hole in the fuselage. Because the hole had changed the aero-dynamics of the huge craft, the usual data regarding stall speed was no longer relevant. The pilot [knowing this] had to use his best judgment. Furthermore, since the plane had just taken on 300,000 pounds of fuel for the long flight, it was too heavy to land without collapsing the landing

gear. . . . Then he encountered a new problem. The wing flaps used to slow down the plane were not working properly. . . . He would have to land the plane at 195 miles per hour, compared to the normal speed of 170 miles per hour. The jet weighed 610,000 pounds, well above Boeing's recommended maximum stress load of 564,000 pounds. Nevertheless, Captain Cronin made one of the smoothest landings the rest of the crew could remember, amid the cheers of the passengers. Airline experts called the landing miraculous. . . . A few days after the harrowing experience, an interviewer asked Captain Cronin about his first thoughts following the loss of the cargo door. He said, "I said a prayer for my passengers momentarily and then got back to business." [82]

Lutheran leader and businessman William Diehl recounts this inspiring story to make an important point. He writes, "If laypeople cannot find any spiritual meaning in their work, they are condemned to living a certain dual life; not connecting what they do on Sunday morning with what they do the rest of the week. They need to discover that the very actions of daily life are spiritual, and enable . . . people to touch God in the world, not away from it. Such a spirituality will say . . . 'Your work is your prayer.'" [83]

So how do we connect what we do on Sunday morning with what we do during the rest of the week? How can we "touch God in the world" through our work? Diehl answers that the very first way to be sure you are serving God in your work is to be competent.

When United Airlines Flight 811 got into trouble, the greatest gift Captain Cronin had for his passengers was his experience and good judgment. In those moments of peril, it mattered not to the passengers how Captain Cronin related to his coworkers or how he communicated his faith to others. . . . The critical issue was this: was he competent enough as a pilot to bring that badly damaged plane in safely. . . . Through our work we can touch God in a variety of ways . . . but if the call of the Christian is to participate in God's ongoing creative process, the bedrock of our ministry has to be *competency*. We must use our talents in as competent a manner as possible.

Competency is a basic value. It is not a means to some other end, such as wealth or position, although such results may occur.[84]

The applications of this dictum—that competent work is a form of love—are many. Those who grasp this understanding of work will still desire to succeed but will not be nearly as driven to overwork or made as despondent by poor results. If it is true, then if you have to choose between work that benefits more people and work that pays you more, you should seriously consider the job that pays less and helps more—particularly if you can be great at it. It means that all jobs—not merely so-called helping professions—are fundamentally ways of loving your neighbor. Christians do not have to do direct ministry or nonprofit charitable work in order to love others through their jobs.

In particular, this principle is one of the main ways for us to find satisfaction in our work, even if our jobs are not, by the world's standards, exciting, high paying, and desirable. Even though, as Luther argues, all work is objectively valuable to others, it will not be subjectively fulfilling unless you consciously see and understand your work as a calling to love your neighbor. John Calvin wrote that "no task will be [seen as] so sordid and base, provided you obey your calling in it, that it will not shine and be reckoned very precious in God's sight."[85] Notice that Calvin speaks of "obey[ing] your calling *in* it"; that is, consciously seeing your job as God's calling and offering the work to him. When you do that, you can be sure that the splendor of God radiates through any task, whether it is as commonplace as tilling a garden, or as rarefied as working on the global trading floor of a bank. As Eric Liddell's missionary father exhorts him in *Chariots of Fire*, "You can praise the Lord by peeling a spud, if you peel it to perfection."

Your daily work is ultimately an act of worship to the God who called and equipped you to do it—no matter what kind of work it is. In the liner notes to his masterpiece *A Love Supreme*, John Coltrane says it beautifully:

> This album is a humble offering to Him. An attempt to say "THANK YOU GOD" through our work, even as we do in our hearts and with our tongues. May He help and strengthen all men in every good endeavor.

PART TWO

Our Problems with Work

FIVE

Work Becomes Fruitless

To the woman he said, "I will make your pains in child-bearing very severe; with painful labor you will give birth to children. Your desire will be for your husband, and he will rule over you."

To Adam he said, "Because you listened to your wife and ate fruit from the tree about which I commanded you, 'You must not eat from it,' cursed is the ground because of you; through painful toil you will eat food from it all the days of your life. It will produce thorns and thistles for you, and you will eat the plants of the field. By the sweat of your brow you will eat your food until you return to the ground, since from it you were taken; for dust you are and to dust you will return."

Genesis 3:16–19

Paradise Lost

We have surveyed the rich biblical view of God's perfect design for work. But that is not how we experience it. Everyone knows that this is a broken, troubled world—shot through with sickness and death, injustice and selfishness, natural disasters, and chaos. Since the beginning of time there has been a wide variety of explanations for why this is so and what to do about it. At the heart of the Bible's account is the concept of sin: man's rebellion against God and our resulting alienation from him. The fall of Adam and Eve (and therefore the rest of the human race) into sin has been disastrous. It has unraveled the fabric of the entire world—and in no area as profoundly as our work. The story presented in the Bible is that while God blessed work to be a glorious use of our gifts and his resources to prosper the world, it is now also cursed because of mankind's fall. Work exists now in a world sustained by God but disordered by sin. Only if we have some understanding of how sin distorts work can we hope to counteract its effects and salvage some of the satisfaction God planned for our work.

In Genesis 2, verse 17, God put Adam and Eve into a garden paradise and told them that if they disobeyed him and ate of a particular tree they would "surely die." What was so special about that one tree? The answer is probably nothing, per se. That is, there was likely nothing magical or unusual about the tree or the fruit itself; the tree was a test. God was saying, "I want you to do something for me, not because you understand why, not because you can see whether it would benefit you or disadvantage you. I want you to obey me, simply because of who I am, simply because you love me and trust me more than anything."

This command, in fact, contained the essence of all the biblical commandments that would be laid out to the nation of Israel, many generations later.[86] It was an opportunity for the human race to voluntarily make our relationship with God the primary value of our lives and to obey his Word simply because it was his due. When Adam and Eve disobeyed this command, they did become "like God," as the serpent (who deceived them into disobedience) said they would. That is, they put themselves in God's place; they took upon themselves the right to decide how they should live and what was right and wrong for them to do. For them to become "like God" in this way was catastrophic. As a sailboat is designed for the water, such that if it runs aground it is damaged and useless, we human beings "run aground" when we choose to be our own source of authority. We were designed to know, serve, and love God supremely—and when we are faithful to that design, we flourish. But when we instead chose to live for ourselves, everything began to work backward. After this turning point the human race began to live against the grain of the universe, against the grain of our own making and purpose.[87] As Paul says in Romans 8, the entire world is now "subject to decay." The poet W.B. Yeats put it this way:

> Things fall apart; the centre cannot hold;
> Mere anarchy is loosed upon the world.[88]

God had warned Adam and Eve that if they ate of the tree, they would die. Most readers assume that God is speaking of immediate physical death, so it is surprising to us when Adam and Eve eat of the tree and they do not slump lifeless to the ground. But that would happen in due course, for eventual physical shutdown is one aspect of the comprehensive death and decay that now comes to every aspect of human life. Nothing works now as it should. Sin leads to the disintegration of *every* area of life: spiritual, physical, social, cultural, psychological, temporal, eternal.

This is important to remember, for many Christians tend to divide the world into "worldly" and "sacred" spaces and activities, as if sin affects only things out in the world; yet absolutely every part of human life—soul and body, private and public, praying and laboring—is affected by sin. Yeats said that "things fall apart," and because of sin they do.

Things Fall Apart

A continued look at Genesis 3 shows that as soon as Adam and Eve sinned against God, they experienced internal shame, guilt, and brokenness. They suffered the natural consequences of working against their design. "They realized they were naked" (verse 7). This is the opposite of verse 25 in chapter 2, where we read that Adam and Eve had been, as we often put it today, "naked and *un*ashamed." Old Testament scholar David Atkinson writes: "Shame . . . is that sense of unease with yourself at the heart of your being."[89] We know there is something wrong with us, but we can't admit it or identify it. There is a deep restlessness, which can take various forms—guilt and striving to prove ourselves, rebellion and the need to assert our independence, compliance and the need to please others. Something is wrong, and we may know the effects, but we fall short of understanding the true causes.

Contemporary Western culture tries to account for this restlessness without recourse to the biblical doctrine of sin. Psychologists help us understand the part our early childhoods have played in creating unnecessary shame or a sense of being unloved. Entertainment distracts us from our discomfort. And doing good helps bolster our identity as a good person. But the Bible locates the root issue as our separation from God.

Another manifestation of this deep unease includes a mistrust and fear of others. The awareness of a need for clothing in the biblical account (verse 7: "they . . . made coverings for themselves") is much more than a new reticence about sex. There was a desire to retreat from what could be called an unself-protective mutuality. Adam and Eve each became desperate to control what the other knew, to hide and create facades to block the other's gaze. This mistrust and fear quickly led to friction and anger, as it now does in all relationships.

In his fascinating interview of Adam and Eve in Genesis 3, verses 10–13, God asks them what has happened. Adam completely avoids the real truth—that he has eaten of the tree—and only complains of his inner unhappiness and shame. God's second question is so direct that Adam cannot avoid naming what he has done, but he immediately deflects the responsibility away from himself to Eve. In turn, Eve deflects to the serpent. Their hostility and anger are directed not only toward other creatures but toward God as well. Adam blames God for his problems— "The woman *you* put here with me—she gave me . . . and I ate. . . ." (verse 12). One commentator on Genesis writes, "In Genesis 3:8 there is an inadequate awareness of the seriousness of sin, moral perceptions are clouded, and the self-centered view of values is well beneath the God-centered view. . . . The blindness of sin is beginning to take effect. . . . From the moment of the fall, humankind has suffered from moral schizophrenia: neither able to deny sinfulness nor to acknowledge it for what it is."[90]

Genesis 3 shows how sin warps every part of our nature, every aspect of human living. It begins by distorting the areas of sex, gender, love, and marriage. God chillingly explains the impact of sin on the relationship between husbands and wives. Scholars debate the exact meaning of God's statement that now, because of sin, "Your desire will be for your husband, and he will rule over you" (verse 16); but all agree it means at least that misunderstanding, frustration, deep conflict, and unhappiness are now the norm in relationships between men and women.[91]

The very fabric of the physical world now began to unravel, and the results are disease, old age, natural disaster, and death itself (Genesis 3:17–19). Philosopher Al Wolters explains it like this:

> The Bible teaches plainly that Adam and Eve's fall into sin was not just an isolated act of disobedience but an event of catastrophic significance for creation as a whole. . . . The effects of sin touch all of creation; no created thing is in principle untouched by the corrosive effects of the fall. Whether we look at societal structures such as the state or family, or cultural pursuits such as art or technology, or bodily functions such as sexuality or eating, or anything at all within the wide scope of creation, we discover that the good handiwork of God has been drawn into the sphere of mutiny against God. "The whole creation," Paul writes, "has been groaning . . . is subject to bondage and decay."[92]

Genesis 3 is an ancient text, filled with rich theology in narrative form. But it could not be more relevant and practical to life today. It goes for the jugular, as if to say, "Do you find the two great tasks in life—love and work—to be excruciatingly hard? This explains why." God ties the pain of love and marriage and the pain of work very closely together in these verses. Both child-bearing and farming are now called "painful labor." Theologian W.R. Forrester writes, "in language after language the same word is used for toil and child-bearing, e.g. 'labor' and 'travail.'"[93] So companies assemble teams to work furiously for months or years to "give birth" to new products or ventures, which may die a quick death in the marketplace. Star football players often suffer the effects of injuries throughout their lives. Brilliant entrepreneurs like Steve Jobs get thrown out of companies when times get tough. (Few get invited back, like Jobs was.) The weeds, or the computer viruses, or the corruption scandals, come back with a vengeance. Research into the properties of the atom becomes the basis for the atomic bomb. In other words, work, even when it bears fruit, is always painful, often miscarries, and sometimes kills us.

Thorns and Thistles

Sin affects not only personal and private life, but also public and social life, and in particular work. As we have seen in Genesis 1 and 2, God made us for work, yet now we learn that work becomes, under sin, "painful toil" (verse 17). Work is not *itself* a curse, but it now lies with all other aspects of human life *under* the curse of sin. "Thorns and thistles" will come up as we seek to grow food (verse 18). When we remember that gardening is representative of all kinds of human labor and culture building, this is a statement that *all* work and human effort will be marked by frustration and a lack of fulfillment. "Part of the curse of work in a fallen world is its frequent fruitlessness."[94]

What do we mean when we say work is fruitless? We mean that, in all our work, we will be able to envision far more than we can accomplish, both because of a lack of ability and because of resistance in the environment around us. The experience of work will include pain, conflict, envy, and fatigue, and not all our goals will be met. For example, you may have an aspiration to do a certain kind of work and perform at a certain level of skill and quality, but you may never even get the opportunity to do the work you want, or if you do, you may not be able to do it as well as it needs to be done. Your conflicts with others in the work environment will sap your confidence and undermine your productivity.

But even during times when you are satisfied with the quality of your work, you may be bitterly disappointed with the results. You may find that circumstances conspire to neutralize any real impact from your project. You may have mastered the skills of farming, but famine or flood or war come in and destroy your harvest. You may have become an accomplished singer, but you are not able to generate an income from your talent because you are skillful in music but not in self-promotion, or because ruthless rivals find ways of blackballing you. And so you have to give up your musical career.

You may hope to make a real contribution to your organization or to work with distinction as an expert in your field. You may aspire to "change the world"—make a major improvement in human society, or have a lasting impact on the culture. Most people achieve very few of these goals in their lifetimes, and even those who seem from a distance to lead charmed work lives will sense that their true aspirations are thwarted as often as they are reached. And for all of us, more often than we would like to admit, we are the ones doing the thwarting.

Imagine you are on a hospital administration team with a vision for making epochal advances in patient care. You make a series of significant changes to how your medical staff sees and treats patients. Initial responses by patients are highly positive, and so are some key metrics on incidence of patient harm, such as blood infections, surgical site infections, and medication errors. But the various new accountability measures—such as department report cards and "safety dashboards"—have many of your medical staff up in arms. They complain that the pressure is too great, the measurements are unfair, and an honest, inadvertent mistake can now ruin a career. You try to reason with many of the staff, but you begin to get defensive. In one staff meeting you lose your cool and say that many staff persons are failing to put the interests of the patients first. There may be some truth in your statement, but it backfires badly. Some are furious with your insinuation. Several of your most respected people leave, and morale takes a sharp dip.

What has happened? Many things. You can look back and see places where you could have been more careful and sensitive to the fears of medical staff. You could have not taken the criticism so personally that you spoke unwisely in some public meetings. So you—and your sin—were part of the problem. You, to put it starkly, were a thorn. The medical staff in many cases *was* simply being stubborn and concerned more about possible blots on their personal records than about the safety of patients. Underneath everything else there is the tragic and seemingly unfair fact of life that in medical facilities, small and virtually unavoidable human errors can ruin or end lives. The thorns and thistles in this situation stem from alienation from others that has its root in the loss of our relationship with God. So even on our best days, each of us is working within a system that feels stacked against us.

I often feel that I have the best job in the world—for me. I am doing what I love to do. We have seen more fruitfulness in our church's ministry than I ever expected to see in a lifetime. But I experience plenty of thorns and thistles. One season I learned I had thyroid cancer and all but the most basic parts of my work were put on hold. My wife has had medical emergencies that thwarted my travel plans or distracted us from new projects. At times staff members have protested that my vision was outpacing my ability to lead it or their ability to implement it. Key leaders in my congregation have moved out of town just as I was ready to entrust some part of the church into their care. I'm grateful to God for the glimpses He's given me of what work was intended to be. But daily I am aware of the maddening encroachment of thorns and thistles in the patch of the world that has been entrusted to me for this season.

Accepting Fruitlessness

One of the most vivid depictions of the frustration and fruitlessness of work is found in Peter Shaffer's play *Amadeus*.[95] Antonio Salieri is court composer to the Hapsburg emperor, and a highly successful writer of operas. He has power and wealth, and yet he senses the mediocrity of what he has produced. Then he meets Mozart and hears his music, and in a flash he stands revealed to himself. He realizes that in Mozart's music he is hearing the beauty he has aspired to create his entire life, but at the same moment, he knows that he will never be capable of producing it himself. As he looks at a written score of Mozart's music, he feels caged, allowed to look through the bars and perceive but not participate in the glory he has hungered for. As he stares at the score, he thinks, "Displace one note and there would be diminishment. Displace one phrase, and the structure would fall. . . . Here . . . was the very voice of God! I was staring through the cage of those meticulous ink-strokes at an absolute, inimitable beauty."[96]

Salieri had to live with the existential frustration of work. That is, despite his dedication and experience, he wasn't as good at composing music as he wanted to be. Yet in terms of outcomes, he was professionally accomplished, achieved high status, and enjoyed financial success. Meanwhile, Mozart was a musical prodigy with abundant gifts, yet he suffered rejection and poverty. Both Mozart and Salieri had success in some aspects of their work lives yet experienced deep frustration in others.

It is important for us to understand and hold in tension what the Bible says about creation and about the fall—about God's plan for work, and also about the problems of work in a broken world. As products of the Depression and two world wars, my parents' and grandparents' generations were grateful to have work of any kind because it helped them and their family survive. But members of my children's generation are utterly dissimilar. They insist that work be fulfilling and fruitful, that it fully fit their talents and their dreams, and that it "do something amazing for the world," as one Google executive described his company's mission.[97] Andy Crouch observes, "We moderns certainly can't be accused of lacking self-confidence. The explosion of books about 'changing the world' fits our self-image."[98] While the circumstances shaping my parents' generation perhaps gave them a lower view of work than the one found in the Bible's description of creation, so my children's generation has a more naïve and utopian view of work than is suggested by the Bible in its description of the world's fall into sin.

In light of all this, was Salieri missing his calling? Should he have taken up work further afield from composition, in the hope that he would not have been as frustrated? I think many contemporary young adults actually might have given him that advice; and they would have been wrong. Salieri was called to contribute to the world as a concert composer—in fact, he produced music that we still have today. The same may well be true to you. Just because you cannot realize your highest aspirations in work does not mean you have chosen wrongly, or are not called to your profession, or that you should spend your life looking for the perfect career that is devoid of frustration. That would be a fruitless search for anyone. You should expect to be regularly frustrated in your work even though you may be in exactly the right vocation.

Nonetheless, was Salieri asking the right questions? Was he justified in longing for an experience of work that might afford him the deep satisfaction of greatness? Of course he was; and while such a line of thought might have seemed self-indulgent to my parents' generation, we know dozens of people for whom those questions led to a new vocation. A young woman in our church was recruited out of college to work on Wall Street. She was one of the leaders of our church's ministry to financial services professionals. Despite success and financial rewards, she made the decision several years into her job that what she really wanted to do with her life was to become a nurse. She walked away from the high salary to go to nursing school and now has begun to practice. In a world where people have on average three to four different careers in their work lives, it is perfectly natural that changing careers may be necessary to maximize fruitfulness. God can—and often does—change what he calls us to do.

Deep Consolation

Because of the nature of God's creation, we need work for our happiness. And because of God's intentions for our work—to contribute to the flourishing of the world—we have glimpses of what we could accomplish. But because of the fall of the human race, our work is also profoundly frustrating, never as fruitful as we want, and often a complete failure. This is why so many people inhabit the extremes of idealism and cynicism—or even ricochet back and forth between those poles. Idealism says, "Through my work I am going to change things, make a difference, accomplish something new, bring justice to the world." Cynicism says, "Nothing really changes. Don't get your hopes up. Do what it takes to make a living. Don't let yourself care too much. Get out of it whatever you can."

Genesis 3, verse 18 tells us not only that "thorns and thistles" will come out of the ground but also that "you will eat the plants of the field." Thorns and food. Work will still bear some fruit, though it will always fall short of its promise. Work will be *both* frustrating and fulfilling, and sometimes—just often enough—human work gives us a glimpse of the beauty and genius that might have been the routine characteristic of all our work, and what, by the grace of God, it will be again in the new heavens and new earth. Tolkien's dream and the resulting story, "Leaf by Niggle," are simply a depiction of this hope. Niggle imagined a beautiful tree that he never was able to produce in paint during his life, so he died weeping that his picture, the great work of his life, was not completed. No one would ever see it. And yet, when he got to the heavenly country—there was the tree! This was Tolkien's way of saying, to us as well as to himself, that our deepest aspirations in work will come to complete fruition in God's future. Just as Niggle's tree survived in all its glory, people will hear Salieri's music, and they will somehow taste the fruit of the project you are working on right now. There will be work in the paradise of the future just like there was in the paradise of the past, because God himself takes joy in his work. In that paradise, you will be useful in the lives of others to infinite degrees of joy and satisfaction; you will perform with all the skill you can imagine.

Christians have, through their hope in God's story of redemption for the world he created, a deep consolation that enables them to work with all their being and never be *ultimately* discouraged by the frustrating present reality of this world, in which thorns grow up when they are trying to coax up other things. We accept the fact that in this world our work will always fall short, just as we sinners always "fall short of the glory of God" (Romans 3:23) because we know that our work in this life is not the final word.

We call upon this consolation every Christmas, though we often do not realize what we are saying:

No more let sin or sorrows grow,
Nor thorns infest the ground;
He comes to make his blessings flow
Far as the curse is found,
Far as the curse is found,
Far as, far as the curse is found.[99]

SIX

Work Becomes Pointless

So I hated life, because the work that is done under the sun was grievous to me. All of it is meaningless, a chasing after the wind.

Ecclesiastes 2:17

Under the Sun

We have seen that work in a fallen world can be fruitless; it can also be pointless. This is another aspect of the alienation human beings sense in their work. That is, while many workers are frustrated by unconsummated skills and unfulfilled aspirations, many others experience no satisfaction or fulfillment in their work even when they *have* realized their aspirations and become successful. One of the most poignant expressions of the way human work can feel so profoundly meaningless comes from a very ancient document, the Old Testament book of Ecclesiastes.

The narrator in the book of Ecclesiastes is called, in Hebrew, Qoheleth, which can be translated as "the Teacher" or perhaps even "the Philosopher." In order to understand what Ecclesiastes has to say about work, however, we need to take a moment to understand the literary genre of the book and how the author gets his points across.

Anyone who reads through Ecclesiastes will be struck by many things that appear to contradict the rest of the Bible. While the Bible everywhere challenges people to live thoroughly wise and righteous lives, Ecclesiastes seems to warn about being "too righteous" or too wicked and commends a middle road—not too moral or too immoral, not too wise or too foolish (Ecclesiastes 7:15–17). How do we explain statements like this?

Old Testament scholar Tremper Longman points out that there was a literary form at that time called "fictional autobiography."[100] In this form, the writer could introduce a fictional character, give a description of his or her life's course, and then conclude with general insights and teachings drawn from the case study of the recounted life. And indeed in Ecclesiastes it is possible to discern two narrators or voices. First the writer of the prologue introduces the fictional character Qoheleth, who in turn speaks in the first person about all the ways he sought to find fulfillment and meaning in life under the sun. The term "under the sun" is crucial to understanding the perspective of the Philosopher. In general, it refers to life in this world considered in and of itself, apart from any greater or eternal reality. The quest of the Philosopher is to have a meaningful life based solely on what can be found within the confines of this material world—achievement, pleasure, and learning.[101] Finally, the original writer speaks in his own voice again and does an evaluation in the epilogue (12:8–14). Thus the writer can dramatize his main themes by depicting the wisest, richest, most gifted man possible, who nonetheless could not find fulfillment in this life.[102]

Some books of the Bible are like listening to a pastor giving counsel on how to live (the book of James in the New Testament, for example, or Proverbs in the Old Testament). But reading Ecclesiastes is like sitting in a philosophy class with a professor who provokes you with thorny Socratic questions and strange case studies, who pulls you into a dialogue to lead you to discover truth for yourself. The Philosopher pushes you to look at the foundations of your life and to ask the basic questions that we might otherwise avoid: "Is there any meaning to your life? What are you really doing it all for? Why is there so much wrong with the world? How will you cope with it?"

The author of Ecclesiastes is using the character of the Philosopher to push readers toward an understanding of the transcendent uniqueness and necessity of God. Nothing within this world is sufficient basis for a meaningful life here. If we base our lives on work and achievement, on love and pleasure, or on knowledge and learning, our existence becomes anxious and fragile—because circumstances in life are always threatening the very foundation of our lives, and death inevitably strips us of everything we hold dear. Ecclesiastes is an argument that existential dependence on a gracious Creator God—not only abstract belief—is a precondition for an unshakeable, purposeful life.

Katherine Alsdorf, like many who make their way to our church well into their careers, can relate to all three of these pursuits: seeking the meaning of life through learning in college, pursuing pleasure and adventure after that, followed by an almost desperate thrust into work and career in her thirties in a full-tilt effort to make life fulfilling. She began to accumulate accomplishments and even some financial prosperity, but grew increasingly stressed and even bitter. She describes her resentment, at the time, of others who were enjoying the fruits of a good life that they hadn't fully earned! Her accomplishments were never enough, and the abundant benefits were never satisfying. As she would put it, "I couldn't handle the idea that it was all meaningless, so I just put my head down and worked harder." Eventually, she started to consider the gospel of Christ because the philosophies of this world were taking her nowhere. The emptiness of life was pushing her toward her own understanding of that transcendent uniqueness of God.

The Meaninglessness of Work

The Philosopher makes his case in stages. The book begins with what has been called three "life projects," each an effort to discover a meaningful life under the sun. The first is a quest to make sense of life through learning and wisdom (Ecclesiastes 1:12–18; 2:12–16). The second is an effort to make life fulfilling through the pursuit of pleasure (2:1–11).

The third project that the Philosopher undertakes to chase away his sense of pointlessness is the pursuit of achievement through hard work (Ecclesiastes 2:17–26). Having tried to live for learning and for pleasure, he now tries to live for the accomplishment of concrete goals and the accrual of wealth and influence. But in the end he concludes that work cannot, all by itself, deliver a meaningful life. "So I hated life, because the work that is done under the sun was grievous to me. All of it is meaningless, a chasing after the wind" (Ecclesiastes 2:17). Why does he draw this conclusion?

When we work, we want to make an impact. That can mean getting personal recognition for our work, or making a difference in our field, or doing something to make the world a better place. Nothing is more satisfying than a sense that through our work we have accomplished some lasting achievement. But the Philosopher startles us by arguing that even if you are one of the few people who breaks through and accomplishes all you hope for, it's all for nothing, for in the end there *are* no lasting achievements. "I hated all the things I had toiled for under the sun, because I must leave them to the one who comes after me. And who knows whether that person will be wise or foolish? Yet they will have control over all the fruit of my toil into which I have poured my effort and skill under the sun. This too is meaningless. So my heart began to despair over all my toilsome labor under the sun" (Ecclesiastes 2:18–20).

Whether quickly or slowly, all the results of our toil will be wiped away by history. The person who takes the business after you, or who picks up the cause or organization after you, may undo all you have done. Of course, some history makers have brought inventions or innovations that stay with the human race for a long time, but those persons are very rare, and of course eventually even the most famous "will not be long remembered" (Ecclesiastes 2:16) since everything and every accomplishment under the sun will be ground to dust in the end—even civilization itself. All work, even the most historic, will eventually be forgotten and its impact totally neutralized (1:3–11).

In short even if your work is not fruitless, it is ultimately pointless if life "under the sun" is all there is.

The Alienation of Work

Work under the sun is meaningless because it does not last; and so it takes away our hope in the future. It also alienates us from God and from one another, so it takes away our joy in the present.

We may again be sympathetic to Antonio Salieri within the narrative of the play *Amadeus*. Here is a man who aspires to create extraordinary music but instead is given modest talents. Being near Mozart shows him how ordinary his music is. He asks God to fill him with creative brilliance, but to no avail. Salieri becomes furious with God. So he says to God, "From now on we are enemies, You and I . . . . Because You will not enter me, with all my need for you; because You scorn my attempts. . . . You are unjust, unfair, unkind. . . ." Salieri turns bitter against God and does what he can to destroy Mozart, God's instrument.

Was God being unfair and unkind? If he was, he wasn't being so only to Salieri. Arguably, only a handful of musicians in all of history have been given gifts like Mozart had. No, Salieri's response was unusually dark and desperate because he had built his entire life on his dream of fame through music. He had begun by trying to put God in his debt:

> Whilst my father prayed earnestly to God to protect commerce, I would offer up secretly the proudest prayer a boy could think of. Lord, make me a great composer! Let me celebrate your glory through music—and be celebrated myself! Make me famous through the world, dear God! Make me immortal! After I die let people speak my name forever with love for what I wrote![103]

The word "immortal" is the key to what was going on in Salieri's heart. His appropriate ambition had become his misplaced salvation; so his considerable success was not enough. He experienced not ordinary disappointment, but alienation and heartbreak, because he was not as good as Mozart.

"What do people get for all the toil and anxious striving with which they labor under the sun? All their days their work is grief and pain; even at night their minds do not rest. This too is meaningless" (Ecclesiastes 2:22–23). Grief and pain so great that he cannot rest: This is the experience of the person whose soul is resting wholly on the circumstances of their work. In this poignant picture, the author is consciously contrasting us with the God whose labor led to real rest (Genesis 2:2), and unconsciously with the Savior who could even sleep through a storm (Mark 4:38).

Another reason that work feels so alienating is the injustice and depersonalization ever-present in all social systems, and which so often infect the nature of work we do. For example, in Ecclesiastes 5, verse 8, Qoheleth says, "If you see the poor oppressed in a district, and justice and rights denied, do not be surprised at such things; for one official is eyed by a higher one, and over them both are others higher still." Old Testament commentator Michael A. Eaton writes of this text that Qoheleth "considers the frustrations of oppressive bureaucracy with its endless delays and excuses . . . and justice is lost between the tiers of the hierarchy."[104] When Qoheleth wrote, only government was a large enough institution to have a bureaucracy, but the last two hundred years have seen the rise of industrialization and the modern corporation. Karl Marx was the first person to speak of "alienated labor" in the heyday of early-nineteenth-century European industry, where "thousands of workers crowded into industrial centers . . . working fourteen hours a day at physically debilitating and mentally stultifying factory jobs . . . [a]t its best, work was a grim form of self-denial for the sake of mere physical survival."[105]

Of course for centuries most people endured backbreaking work just to survive, yet at least in small farms or shops it was possible to see the product of one's work. But in a factory, a worker might be tasked to put five nuts onto wheel lugs every thirty seconds, hour after hour, day after day. In his book *Working,* Studs Terkel interviewed many industrial workers, including Mike, who put steel parts onto a rack, lowered them into a vat of paint that bonded to their surfaces, and then raised and unloaded the rack. That was all he did. "'Put it on, take it off, put it on, take it off,' he reports. 'In between I don't even try to think. . . .' His job is typical of manufacturing work or even office work which has been subdivided and simplified for the sake of efficiency and higher productivity."[106]

The great shift from an industrial economy to a knowledge and service economy has improved the immediate working conditions of many but has locked countless others into low-paying service sector jobs that experience the same alienating disconnection from the fruits or products of their work.[107] And even in many areas such as finance, where workers make far more than "sweatshop" wages, the size and complexity of global corporations now makes it difficult for even high-ranking executives to understand what their labor is producing. A banker in a small town making mortgage and small business loans can easily see the purpose and fruit of her labor. A bank worker bundling thousands of subprime loans and buying and selling them in enormous blocks of capital will have more difficulty answering the question, "What is your work for?"

Work can even isolate us from one another. "There was a man all alone; he had neither son nor brother. There was no end to his toil, yet his eyes were not content with his wealth. 'For whom am I toiling,' he asked, 'and why am I depriving myself of enjoyment?' This too is meaningless—a miserable business!" (Ecclesiastes 4:7–8). This man is "alone"—without friends or family—as a result of his work. Work can convince you that you are working hard for your family and friends while you are being seduced through ambition to neglect them. Work involves "depriving"—delayed gratification and sacrifice. But he asks, "For *whom* am I toiling and depriving myself of enjoyment?" In the end, he finds that working for his own sake is unrewarding. Commentator Derek Kidner adds: "This picture of lonely, pointless busyness . . . checks any excessive claim we might wish to make for the blessings of hard work."[108]

The Danger of Choice

Ecclesiastes says, "A person can do nothing better than to . . . find satisfaction in their own toil" (2:24). One of the reasons so many people find work to be unsatisfying is, ironically, that people today have more power to choose their line of work than did people in the past. Recently David Brooks wrote in *The New York Times* about an online discussion conducted by a Stanford professor with students and recent graduates about why so many students from the most exclusive universities go into either finance or consulting. Some defended their pathways; others complained that "the smartest people should be fighting poverty, ending disease and serving others, not themselves."[109] Brooks said that while the discussion was illuminating, he was struck by the unspoken assumptions.

> Many of these students seem to have a blinkered view of their options. There's crass but affluent investment banking. There's the poor but noble nonprofit world. And then there is the world of high-tech start-ups, which magically provides money and coolness simultaneously. But there was little interest in or awareness of the ministry, the military, the academy, government service or the zillion other sectors. Furthermore, few students showed any interest in working for a company that actually makes products. . . .
>
> [C]ommunity service has become a patch for morality. Many people today have not been given vocabularies to talk about what virtue is, what character consists of, and in which way excellence lies, so they just talk about community service. . . . In whatever field you go into, you will face greed, frustration and failure. You may find your life challenged by depression, alcoholism, infidelity, your own stupidity and self-indulgence. . . . Furthermore . . . [a]round what ultimate purpose should your life revolve? Are you capable of heroic self-sacrifice or is life just a series of achievement hoops? . . . You can devote your life to community service and be a total schmuck. You can spend your life on Wall Street and be a hero. Understanding heroism and schmuck-dom requires fewer Excel spreadsheets, more Dostoyevsky and the Book of Job.[110]

Brooks's first point is that so many college students do not choose work that actually fits their abilities, talents, and capacities, but rather choose work that fits within their limited imagination of how they can boost their own self-image. There were only three high-status kinds of jobs—those that paid well, those that directly worked on society's needs, and those that had the cool factor. Because there is no longer an operative consensus on the dignity of all work, still less on the idea that in all work we are the hands and fingers of God serving the human community, in their minds they had an extremely limited range of career choices. That means lots of young adults are choosing work that doesn't fit them, or fields that are too highly competitive for most people to do well in. And this sets many people up for a sense of dissatisfaction or meaninglessness in their work.

Perhaps it is related to the mobility of our urban culture and the resulting disruption of community, but in New York City many young people see the process of career selection more as the choice of an identity marker than a consideration of gifting and passions to contribute to the world. One young man explained, "I chose management consulting because it is filled with sharp people—the kind of people I want to be around." Another said, "I realized that if I stayed in education, I'd be embarrassed when I got to my five-year college reunion, so I'm going to law school now." Where one's identity in prior generations might come from being the son of so-and-so or living in a particular part of town or being a member of a church or club, today young people are seeking to define themselves by the status of their work.

What wisdom, then, would the Bible give us in choosing our work? First, if we have the luxury of options, we would want to choose work that we can do well. It should fit our gifts and our capacities. To take up work that we can do well is like cultivating our *selves* as gardens filled with hidden potential; it is to make the greatest room for the ministry of competence. Second, because the main purpose of work is to serve the world, we would want to choose work that benefits others. We have to ask whether our work or organization or industry makes people better or appeals to the worst aspects of their characters. The answer will not always be black and white; in fact, the answer could differ from person to person. In a volume on the Christian approach to vocation, John Bernbaum and Simon Steer presented the case of Debbie, a woman who made a great deal of money working for an interior-decorating company in Aspen, Colorado. The craft of interior design, like architecture or the arts, is as positive way to promote human well-being. But she often found herself using resources in ways that she could not reconcile with pursuing the common good. She left her career to work for a church and later for a U.S. senator. Debbie said, "Not that there was anything dishonest or illegal involved, but I was being paid on a commission basis—thirty percent of the gross profit. One client spent twenty thousand dollars [in the early 1980s] on furnishings for a ten-by-twelve [foot] room. I began to question my motivation for encouraging people to . . . spend huge sums of money on furniture. So . . . I decided to leave."[111] This example is not about the value of the interior design profession or the commission form of compensation. Rather, it illustrates the need for everyone to work out in clear personal terms how their work serves the world.

Someone else in the same situation might have chosen to stay, to focus on helping clients create beautiful homes, and to see the commissions as a legitimate expression of the value of that beauty.

Third, if possible, we do not simply wish to benefit our family, benefit the human community, and benefit ourselves—we also want to benefit our field of work itself. In Genesis 1 and 2, we saw that God not only cultivated his creation, but he created more cultivators. Likewise, our goal should not simply be to do work, but to increase the human race's capacity to cultivate the created world. It is a worthy goal to want to make a contribution to your discipline, if possible; to show a better, deeper, fairer, more skillful, more ennobling way of doing what you do. Dorothy Sayers explores this point in her famous essay "Why Work?" She acknowledges that we should work for "the common good" and "for others" (as we observed in chapter 4), but she doesn't want us to stop there. She says that the worker must "serve the work."[112]

> The popular catchphrase of today is that it is everybody's duty to serve the community, but . . . there is, in fact, a paradox about working to serve the community, and it is this: that to aim directly at serving the community is to falsify the work. . . . There are . . . very good reasons for this:
>
> [T]he moment you [only] think of serving other people, you begin to have a notion that other people owe you something for your pains; you begin to think that you have a claim on the community. You will begin to bargain for reward, to angle for applause, and to harbor a grievance if you are not appreciated. But if your mind is set upon serving the work, then you know you have nothing to look for; the only reward the work can give you is the satisfaction of beholding its perfection. The work takes all and gives nothing but itself; and to serve the work is a labor of pure love.

The only true way of serving the community is to be truly in sympathy with the community, to be oneself part of the community and then to *serve the work*. . . . It is the work that serves the community; the business of the worker is to serve the work.[113]

Sayers's point is well taken and not often made or understood. It is possible to imagine you are "serving the community" because what you do is popular—at least for a time. However, you may no longer be serving the community—you may be using it for the way its approval makes you feel. But if you do your work so well that by God's grace it helps others who can never thank you, or it helps those who come after you to do it better, then you know you are "serving the work," and truly loving your neighbor.

A Handful of Quietness

In the midst of Qoheleth's gloom regarding the pointlessness of work, a couple of gleams shine through. "There is nothing better for a person than to enjoy their work, because that is their lot" (Ecclesiastes 3:22). Yes, work is our inescapable "lot," and so satisfaction in that realm is essential to a satisfactory life. But how do we get that satisfaction in light of all that we have against us? The answer: "to . . . find satisfaction in all their toil—this is the gift of God" (Ecclesiastes 3:13). How can we secure this gift? Qoheleth provides a hint.

Fools fold their hands and ruin themselves.
Better one handful with tranquility
than two handfuls with toil and chasing after the wind.
Ecclesiastes 4:5–6

Qoheleth commends, literally, "one handful of quietness"—by contrast with two alternatives. One is the "two handfuls" of wealth that come from "toil and chasing after the wind" (verse 6b). The other is the "empty handful" of wealth that comes from the idleness of the fool who does not toil at all (verse 5). Qoheleth concedes that satisfaction in work in a fallen world is always a miraculous gift of God—and yet we have a responsibility to pursue this gift through a particular balance. Tranquility without toil will not bring us satisfaction; neither will toil without tranquility. There will be both toil *and* tranquility.

How we attain such a balanced life is one of the main themes of Scripture. First, it means recognizing and renouncing our tendency to make idols of money and power (see Ecclesiastes 4:4— "I saw that all toil and all achievement spring from one person's envy of another. This too is meaningless, a chasing after the wind"). Second, it means putting relationships in their proper place (see Ecclesiastes 4:8—"There was a man all alone; he had neither son nor brother"), even though it probably means making less money ("one handful" rather than two).

But most of all, it will mean pursuing something that is beyond the scope of Ecclesiastes to identify. The New Testament reveals that the ultimate source of the tranquility we seek is Jesus Christ, who—because he has toiled for us on the cross—can offer us the true rest for our souls (Matthew 11:28–30). Without the gospel of Jesus, we will have to toil not for the joy of serving others, nor the satisfaction of a job well done, but to make a name for ourselves.

SEVEN

Work Becomes Selfish

As people moved eastward, they found a plain in Shinar and settled there. They said to each other, "Come, let's make bricks and bake them thoroughly." They used brick instead of stone, and tar for mortar. Then they said, "Come, let us build ourselves a city, with a tower that reaches to the heavens, so that we may make a name for ourselves; otherwise we will be scattered over the face of the whole earth."

Genesis 11:2–4

Making a Name for Ourselves

One of the reasons work is both fruitless and pointless is the powerful inclination of the human heart to make work, and its attendant benefits, the main basis of one's meaning and identity. When this happens, work is no longer a way to create and bring out the wonders of the created order, as Calvin would say, or to be an instrument of God's providence, serving the basic needs of our neighbor, as Luther would say. Instead it becomes a way to distinguish myself from my neighbor, to show the world and prove to myself that I'm special. It is a way to accumulate power and security, and to exercise control over my destiny. So often the observation of Qoheleth holds true—"I saw that all labor and achievement spring from man's envy of his neighbor. This too is meaningless, a chasing after the wind" (Ecclesiastes 4:4).

Nowhere is the shift from work as grateful stewardship of our gifts to neurotic fabrication of our self-worth more evident than in the first eleven chapters of Genesis. In Genesis 1 and 2, work is a joyful cultivation of creation for its own sake and God's sake (Genesis 1:28, 2:15). By Genesis 4, technology has become a means to power. In Genesis 11, we come to the famous story of the building of the Tower of Babel.

Two reasons are given for the building of the Tower. In verse 3 the people of Shinar say, "'let's make bricks and bake them thoroughly' . . . instead of stone . . ." Someone had discovered a way of making bricks that was an advance beyond previous methods of building. It meant they could build a much taller building than had ever been built before. They wanted to take their new talents and discoveries to use them in a big city. Ever since then, the people with the most creative new ideas continue to seek out cities to find a fertile environment for experimentation and implementation of their dreams. So far, so good.

But there is a second, deeper reason for their project of city building: "so that we may make a name for ourselves; otherwise we will be scattered over the face of the whole earth" (verse 4). What were the builders of the tower doing their work for? What are most of today's ambitious workers doing *their* work for? Verse 4 tells us vividly—and the motivation has not changed from that day to this one. It was to maximize their power, glory, and autonomy. Yet even this boast reveals their radical insecurity.

They built the city to "make a name for [them]selves" through their accomplishments—but if we lack a name, it means we don't know who we are. "To make a name" in the language of the Bible is to construct an identity for ourselves. We either *get* our name—our defining essence, security, worth, and uniqueness—from what God has done for us and in us (Revelation 2:17), or we *make* a name through what we can do for ourselves. Old Testament scholar Derek Kidner writes, "The elements of the story are timelessly characteristic of the spirit of the world. The project is typically grandiose; men describe it excitedly to one another as if it were the ultimate achievement. . . . At the same time they betray their insecurity as they crowd together to preserve their identity and control their fortunes."[114]

There seem to be two ways that the people of Babel are getting their identity from their work. First, the grandiose statement "a tower that reaches to the heavens" suggests that they are assigning spiritual value to their work that they would be better off getting from God. This leads to materialism, as we allow the fruits of our labor to tell us we are healthy and safe. Second, the desire not to "be scattered over the face of the whole earth" seems to mean that they also get a name from being gathered into a large group. Part of their sense of power and security comes from the size and wealth of their city. While the first kind of identity-making comes from creating an idol of one's *individual* talents and accomplishments, the second kind comes from making an idol of one's *group*. This leads, of course, to snobbery, imperialism, colonialism, and various other forms of racism.

In the final scene of this brief story, God comes down in judgment on the city, but observe the form of his punishment. Were it a Hollywood special effects blockbuster, he might send lightning and earthquakes to destroy the settlement. Instead, he "confuses their language" so that they fall into disunity and scatter. Here we see a principle that runs throughout the Bible: Sin has natural consequences. The desires of the sinful heart create strains in the fabric of the real world that always lead to breakdown. Our pride and need for personal significance necessarily lead to competition, disunity, and strife. So a life of self-glorification makes unity and love between people impossible. It leaves us with the dreary choice between making the self an idol (which leads to the disunity of individualistic cultures) and making the group to an idol (which leads to the suppression of individual freedom in tribal or collective cultures). The two things we all want so desperately—glory and relationship—can coexist only with God.

Babel is a pointed case study of the impossibility of building any collective endeavor—a society, an organization, a movement—that really "works" unless it is grounded beyond itself, in God. Every other society will have to make an idol out of something that will ultimately disappoint. The family, or the individual self, or national pride, or the accruing of personal wealth—something other than God—will end up being considered the bottom line, the *summum bonum,* the giver of the name. As Derek Kidner puts it, "The half-built city is all too apt a monument to this aspect of man."[115]

The people of Shinar wanted to build the tallest building in the world. This peculiar project of humankind has shown no signs of abating for many millennia, and it seems that every year we hear of a building going up somewhere that will make a name for someone new and stand as the world's tallest for a time. This is a vivid example of the spirit of competitive pride that drives the work in every field. Of course, there is something very useful in this dynamic—it stimulates helpful innovation and efficiencies—but there is also something pernicious in it.

See how C.S. Lewis puts it in *Mere Christianity*:

> Now what I want you to get clear is that Pride is essentially competitive—is competitive by its very nature. . . . Pride gets no pleasure out of having something, only out of having more of it than the next man. We say people are proud of being rich, or clever, or good-looking but they are not. They are proud of being richer, or cleverer, or better-looking than others.[116]

Lewis shows us that we can either build a better mousetrap (taller building, faster computer, cheaper airline, more luxurious hotel) out of interest in excellence and service to human beings, or we can do so in a race to move our organization and ourselves into a position to look down on others. The latter leads to ethical shortcuts and the oppression of those who get in our way.

I want to make it clear at this point that no one can live entirely out of the pure impulse to serve the interests of other people at all times. Even the most loving, morally beautiful people fall prey to motives of self-interest, fear, and glory seeking. Our acceptance of our own brokenness—and the world's—keeps us going back to God to remember what we cannot do on our own. As a matter of fact, it is very dangerous to think of certain people as being "the good ones" who work to serve and of others as "the bad ones" who are seeking to prove and serve themselves. The DNA of self-centeredness and competitive pride are at work deep in each of us.

The Power of Being "in the Palace"

An extended case study on the themes of self-interest, power, and vocation can be found in the Old Testament book of Esther. The book recounts an incident when the Jews were dispersed throughout the Persian Empire. In the first chapter we are told how the Persian emperor, King Xerxes, has disposed of his queen Vashti because she was too bold and displeased him. He looks for another queen and discovers Esther, a beautiful young Jewish girl. He sleeps with her and she pleases him. Esther hides her Jewish identity as she is elevated to be his queen in the royal palace.

Almost all readers of this story are offended by this early part of the book of Esther. Feminist interpreters are outraged at Esther's subservience. Others are offended by the fact that unlike Daniel, who identified himself as a Jew and lived as one publicly in a pagan court, Esther keeps quiet. People of traditional moral views are bothered that she sleeps with a man to whom she is not married. Through all these moral compromises, she rises to a place near the center of power. So we are posed with a question: In such morally, culturally, and spiritually ambiguous situations, does God still work with us and through us? The answer of the book is yes.

At the beginning of the fourth chapter of the book of Esther—the start of act two, in a sense—we learn that Haman, a high official, has convinced the king that the Jews are a danger to the empire and has secured a royal decree that on a future date, neighbors of Jewish families throughout the realm will be free to kill them and plunder their wealth (Esther 3:1–15). Esther's relative Mordecai, a Jewish leader, contacts Esther and tells her she must use her place in the palace to avert this danger. This is a huge request. Here a believer in God, whose place of power in the public sphere is tenuous, is being called to use her personal and cultural capital to bring about a more just social order. "Who knows," Mordecai says to her, "but that you have come to your royal position for such a time as this?" (Esther 4:14).

The book of Esther parallels the biblical accounts of Daniel and Joseph. All three people were believers in the God of Israel. Each was an official in a pluralistic, nonbelieving government and culture. None were prophets, priests, elders, or teachers. They had reached the highest circles of power in their secular cultural institutions. And God used them mightily.

Dick Lucas, an English Anglican preacher, once preached a sermon on the story of Joseph. What he said fits in well with this account of Esther. He said that if you were to go to a book table at a church and see a biography with the title *The Man God Uses* or *The Woman God Uses*, you would immediately think it was the story of a missionary, teacher, church leader, or specialist in some sort of spiritual work. He points out that what you have in the story of Joseph is a highly successful secular official. Lucas says, "In the long term I think being a preacher, missionary, or leading a Bible study group in many ways is easier. There is a certain spiritual glamour in doing it, and what we should be doing each day is easier to discern more black and white, not so gray. It is often hard to get Christians to see that God is willing not just to use men and women in ministry, but in law, in medicine, in business, in the arts. This is the great shortfall today."[117]

We have a perfect example in this story. Since Jerusalem was destroyed by Nebuchadnezzar, the Jews have been in exile. At this point in biblical history, they are on their way back. They are trying to rebuild their lives, their city, and their nation. Ray Bakke, an academic and writer, points out that God shows the diversity of the people he uses by giving us three different books in the Bible describing how he restores the nation of Israel back to its homeland.[118] First, the book of Ezra is about a minister, a teacher of the word. The Jews needed to be reacquainted with the Bible so their lives could be shaped by what God said. Second, the book of Nehemiah is about an urban planner and developer who used his management skills to rebuild the wall of Jerusalem and reinstate stability so that economic and civic life could begin to flourish again. Last, the book of Esther is about a woman with power in the civil government working against racial injustice. Here you have male and female, lay and clergy. You have people working for spiritual maturity, economic flourishing, and better public policy, in cultures that defined and valued these ideas differently from the Jews. And God is using them all.

Don't be too quick to miss the connection between Esther and us. I remember some years ago hearing a Hispanic pastor preaching on the book of Esther. Many of his older church members had been immigrants and had little money or clout, but many of the younger generation had gone to college and had become professionals. The preacher told them that even though they didn't see it, they were "in the palace." They had more financial and cultural capital than they realized. And, he said in no uncertain terms, many of them were using that capital to feather their own nests and move ahead in their own careers rather than leveraging it for others. He reminded them that there were poorer people across the city who needed their connections and talents. He said that inside their circles of influence and fields of work there was corruption that needed their attention. He admitted that if his listeners conducted themselves in that way, they might make less money or move up the ladder slower or run into conflict that could hurt their careers. But that doesn't matter, he said. Don't just get into the palace and bend every rule you can to stay there. Serve. *You have come to your royal position for such a time as this.*

I know some of us feel like Esther. There is the VP of an investment bank who has kept many of his investors in the dark—maybe only passively. There is the football coach who violates a number of NCAA recruiting rules. There is the municipal official who doesn't take bribes but looks the other way when she sees colleagues who do. In part because of these compromises, they have all risen and now occupy high positions; but their consciences are not clear. You may be like them, on a smaller or larger scale. You may have made some choices that were unethical or very much in the "gray area." You may have been asked to repeatedly tell clients that the work was done in a certain way when you knew it wasn't. You may not have spoken out when you knew you should have. You have some clout now, but you don't feel as though your conscience is clear. Do you think Esther's conscience was clear? Is anyone's ever completely clear? It is never too late. God urges you to think about where you are and why you are there, to realize the importance of being in the palace. It's possible that only then can He use you to do His work in this world.

I have a friend who worked in private equity at a major financial services firm. We asked him to teach a class on character and integrity in our church. During the class he shared a recent dilemma in which the team who worked for him identified an excellent investment opportunity that would provide a good return for his team and the company. The only problem was that the business in my friend's mind, not only didn't make a positive contribution to society but damaged it. It wasn't illegal, and the firm itself had no issue with investing in this business. He was torn between his obligation to create the highest value for his own company and staff, and his faith-based commitment to human flourishing. He could veto the investment, but that would only put the deal in the hands of a competing bank. He could agree to the investment and profit from something that he didn't believe in. He wanted to at least take a stand and live out his convictions in some way. So he announced to his team that he would not veto the deal, but he would personally choose to not participate in any bonus that might result from their investment. That gave him the opportunity to explain his rationale and present a picture of God's intentions for human flourishing. The deal closed, and the investment made the bank a lot of money. But what of my friend's sacrifice? He took an opportunity, at a true cost to himself, to take a stand and point to his colleagues an alternate vision of life in the palace.

The Peril of Being "in the Palace"

Esther's concern was very real; Mordecai was asking her to take an enormous risk. In that time and place, to fall out of favor with the king did not mean losing your job; it more often meant losing your life. Esther replies to Mordecai that it was a capital offense for anyone to go in to the king unbidden, ". . . unless the king extends the gold scepter to them and spares their lives. But thirty days have passed since I was called to go to the king" (Esther 4:11). Surely Esther is remembering that the last queen was deposed because she was too bold! Mordecai doesn't know what he is asking of her; she could lose everything.

Mordecai responds that indeed he does know. He steps up to the high point of the story rhetorically, narratively, and theologically: "Do not think that because you are in the king's house you alone of all the Jews will escape. For if you remain silent at this time, relief and deliverance for the Jews will arise from another place, but you and your father's family will perish" (Esther 4:13–14). Mordecai is saying that if Esther risks losing the palace, she *might* lose everything, but if she doesn't risk losing the palace, she *will* lose everything. It is an agonizing argument. If all the Jews are killed, Esther will be sniffed out and killed. If the Jews are not killed, Esther will be considered a traitor. Mordecai then closes with hope: "And who knows but that you have come to your royal position for such a time as this?" (verse 14). What Mordecai says has direct application for most of us.

Mordecai, in effect, appeals to the idea of vocation. He says the same thing the Hispanic pastor said: Unless you use your clout, your credentials, and your money in service to the people outside the palace, the palace is a prison; it has already given you your name. You may think you have been given little because you are always striving for more, but you have been given much, and God has called you to put it into play. It is natural to root your identity in your position in the palace; to rest your security in the fact that you have a certain measure of control over the variables in your life; to find your significance in having clout in certain circles. But if you are unwilling to risk your place in the palace for your neighbors, the palace owns you.

How do you get a new name, based on something other than the palace? The text hints at the answer: grace. Mordecai says to

Esther, "Who knows but that you have come to your royal position for such a time as this?" The Hebrew word translated as "come" is a passive verb. It would be better translated: "Who knows but that you were not *brought* to your royal position because of this?" He is reminding Esther that she did not get to the palace except by grace. She did not develop or earn her beauty, nor did she produce this opportunity; they were given to her. Have you contemplated how much this is true of you too? If someone claims that your professional status is a result of grace, you immediately think they don't know how hard you worked to get into your school, how hard you worked in school and at your internships, how you have performed better than your peers at work, and so on. However, you worked with talents you did not earn; they were given to you. You went through doors of opportunity you did not produce; they just opened for you. Therefore, everything you have is a matter of grace, and so you have the freedom to serve the world through your influence, just as you can through your competence.

Living with Greatness in the Palace

Esther begins to respond. The Esther we know from chapters 1 and 2—the demure beauty queen who lies about her race to stay on the inside track—begins to fade away. The Esther who never rocks the boat and never ruffles any feathers starts to give orders. She sends a message to Mordecai: "Go, gather together all the Jews who are in Susa, and fast for me. Do not eat or drink for three days, night or day. I and my attendants will fast as you do. When this is done, I will go to the king, even though it is against the law. And if I perish, I perish" (Esther 4:16).

What happens next is one of the most absorbing narrative accounts in the Bible. By a series of "coincidences"—of course, they are anything but—as well as Esther's own courage, she is received by the king and is able to unmask the hatred and calculation of Haman so that Haman is executed and the Jewish people saved.

But it would be a mistake to end the account here. There is a danger that you might merely be inspired by Esther's example. You look at Esther and decide you are not going to look at your position and your intellectual, social, and financial capital in a new way. Instead of looking at your influence as a means to move yourself ahead, you are going to use it to serve people; you are going to take more risk to see that justice is done. Or you may decide that you have been too quiet about your beliefs, so you resolve to speak up and let people know what you believe. Those are good and right impulses; by all means follow them.

Yet they aren't enough. To begin with, your resolve won't last. If you are merely inspired by an example—you want to be like Esther, or you want to be more like the people the Hispanic pastor said we needed—then your basic motivation is probably guilt. It could be guilt over selfishness, guilt over elitism, even guilt over ungratefulness. And those may be the right place to start! But if guilt is the extent of your motivation, you can be sure it will wear off before long because living in a new way will be hard.

Or, you might get inspired, but overreact. So often I have seen people who have previously kept secret about their faith and who overcompensate and become obnoxious. They decide to be an outspoken, principled person; they will not be like "those closeted Christians." Yet they haven't really left the palace because they are still getting their identity from their performance of a "better" kind of Christianity. They have not really changed; they are very self-righteously being more overt.

Let me suggest how you are more likely to live with integrity, even greatness, in the palace. Look at Esther not merely as an example but as a signpost, a pointer. You see, God created us, he gave us everything we have, and he sustains our life every moment; therefore, we owe him everything. But we do not live that way. We live as if everything we have is ours, to use as we see fit, to make our own name. Even people who do not consider themselves Christians know, on reflection, that something is wrong with this picture. By everyone's standards, we are violating our relationship with God. The religions of the world disagree on the story and the reasons, but they all agree on something: There is a gap—or a chasm—between the divine and us. Some religions say we must cross that divide through sacrifice, rituals, transformation of consciousness, or ethical practice. But somehow we need something to bridge that gap between God and ourselves. How will we find it?

Here's the answer of the Bible, right from this story. Esther saved her people through *identification and mediation*. Her people were condemned, but she identified with them and came under that condemnation. She risked her life and said, "If I perish, I perish." Because she identified, she could mediate before the throne of power as no one else could, and because she received favor there, that favor was transferred to her people. Saving people through identification and mediation—does that remind you of anyone? Jesus Christ, the Son of God, lived in the ultimate palace with ultimate beauty and glory, and he voluntarily left them behind. Philippians 2 says that he had equality with the Father, but he did not hold on to it; instead, he emptied himself, identified with us, and took on our condemnation. He did not do it at the risk of his life but at the cost of his life. He didn't say, "*If* I perish, I perish," but "*When* I perish, I'll perish." He went to the Cross and died; he made atonement for our sins. Now he stands before the throne of the universe, and the favor he has procured is ours if we believe in him. His is ultimate mediation.

If you see Esther not as an example but as a pointer to Jesus, and if you see Jesus not as an example but as a Savior doing these things for you personally, then you will see how valuable you are to him. Meditate on these things, and the truth will change your identity. It will convince you of your real, inestimable value. And ironically, when you see how much you are loved, your work will become far less selfish. Suddenly all the other things in your work life—your influence, your résumé, and the benefits they bring you—become just things. You can risk them, spend them, and even lose them. You are free. Esther was able to do what she did merely on the basis of a vague revelation that God is a god of grace. But now we know so much more! She didn't know God was actually going to come to earth himself and do what she was doing on an infinitely greater scale, at an infinitely greater cost, with infinitely greater benefits to humanity. We now know so much more about his grace, our value to him, and our future.

If you see what Jesus Christ has done for you, losing the ultimate palace for you, then you will be able to start to serve God and your neighbor from your place in the palace. Karen Jobes, who wrote a commentary on the book of Esther, says Esther is called *Queen* Esther fourteen times; thirteen of those happen af-

ter she says, "If I perish, I perish."[119] She becomes a person of greatness not by trying to make a name for herself; and you will become a person of greatness not by trying to make yourself into one, but by serving the One who said to his Father, "For your sake, thy will be done."

EIGHT

Work Reveals Our Idols

Do not make any idols.

Exodus 34:17

The Pervasiveness and Power of Idols

David closeted himself in his corner office while his new board of directors considered his demands. "I'll make them come to me," he thought, leaning on the negotiating techniques he had learned over the course of a very successful career. In two decades David had risen to become CEO of a series of increasingly high-profile technology companies, and the previous week had been one of those great moments of payoff. Flying high at dinner after the analyst call announcing the sale of his latest company to a nationally known enterprise, he said to his associate, "This is it! It doesn't get any better than this! This is what it's all about!"

But now it was time to exit and move on to the next opportunity. While the payout from this deal was respectable—a valuation of three times annual earnings and a nice round million dollars in his pocket—it was really only a stepping-stone to a bigger venture. He'd done what he was brought in to do—sell the company before the technology was displaced by another one and give the investors a good return on their dollar.

His thoughts floated to the million dollars. His wife wanted a beach house, he wanted a lake house; their exquisite home had just been renovated, and the kids were doing well. They'd also been able to buy homes for each of their parents, nearby and in good neighborhoods. David felt good about the way he'd been able to support his family. This was important to him.

Years ago, as his father struggled with work, and money for the family was extremely tight, he'd vowed to himself that his life would be different. He'd use the opportunities his parents had given him, modest as they might be, to make something of himself. It would be a way to honor his father, now passed away. And his children would never have to want for anything. Yet his mom was already saying, "So, David, you have enough already. Do you really have to find the next bigger and better company? What's behind all this drive?"

At that point, the door opened, and the board member he'd worked with most closely on the deal walked in. Sitting down, he said, "David, we really need you to honor your contract and stay the full year; the company needs you to lead it right now. You were one of the key reasons we thought buying the company was a good deal—you're smart, you're a good leader, you can negotiate partnerships and deals to keep this company out front. We can't agree to letting you out now."

David loathed the prospect of staying on for another year and was determined to get the full payout in spite of the terms of the contract. He held the ultimate card: They certainly wouldn't want to keep him if he made it clear that he didn't want to stay. No one can lead well if his heart isn't in it, right?

A week later, having refused to budge on any point, he walked away with the payout and very quickly moved into the corner office of a Fortune 500 company.

When contemporary people hear the word "idols" they are most likely to think of the entertainment world, where celebrities are called "teen idols" or where aspirants compete to be the next "American Idol." Or perhaps the word conjures thoughts of primitive people bowing down to figurines and images. If the word is ever connected to the world of work, it is usually a rhetorical device to say someone has become a workaholic or is rapaciously greedy, so that success or money has become an object of extreme devotion. These are all legitimate uses of the term, but they are only the most extreme cases of the powerful and pervasive conception that is at the heart of biblical faith. The most famous and influential moral code in the world, the Ten Commandments, begins with God's great directive on idolatry: "You shall have no other gods before me" (Exodus 20:3).

What does it mean to have other gods? The commandment says: "You shall not make for yourself an image in the form of anything in heaven above or on the earth beneath or in the waters below. You shall not bow down to them or worship them. . . ." (Exodus 20:4–5). We have an alternate or counterfeit god if we take anything in creation and begin to "bow down" to it—that is, to love, serve, and derive meaning from it more than from the true God. Because we can set up idols in our hearts (Ezekiel 14:3–7), we recognize that "making an image" of something is not necessarily a physical process but is certainly a spiritual and psychological one. It means imagining and trusting anything to deliver the control, security, significance, satisfaction, and beauty that only the real God can give. It means turning a good thing into an ultimate thing.

Many have recognized the significance of the Bible's command against idolatry, placed at the very beginning of God's directions for life. No one grasped its power more than Martin Luther. He defined idolatry as looking to some created thing to give you what only God can give you. Therefore, he argued, even nonreligious people serve "gods"—ideologies or abilities that they believe can justify their lives. French philosopher Luc Ferry, himself a nonbeliever in God, likewise argues that everyone seeks "some way to face life with confidence, and death without fear and regret." All of us look to something to assure ourselves we have spent our lives well. David, in our opening example, may have sought financial security money and success as his "salvation" from the struggle of his childhood, although he would never have used that term. Whatever it is we seek, Ferry says, it is a form of salvation.[120] This fits with the implication of the first of the Ten Commandments. God says, "I am the Lord your God; you shall have no other gods before me." Notice that God says that either *he* will be our God or something else will. He leaves open no in-between possibility of having no gods at all that we rely on to "save" us.

Luther saw how harmoniously the concept of idolatry tied the Old and New Testaments together. The Old Testament talks about idolatry a great deal, while the New Testament, especially the letters of Paul, speaks about union with Christ and justification by faith—means through which we are saved by God's grace rather than by our own efforts. Luther came to realize that these two ideas—to set up an idol and to try to save yourself through your own efforts—are describing essentially the same thing. In his *Treatise Concerning Good Works*, Luther wrote:

> The First Commandment commands: "Thou shalt have no other gods," which means: "Since I alone am God, thou shalt place all thy confidence trust and faith on Me alone, and on no one else." . . . All those who do not at all times trust God and . . . His favor, grace and good-will, but seek His favor in other things or in themselves, do not keep this Commandment, and practice real idolatry. . . . If we do not believe that God is gracious to us and is pleased with us, or if we presumptuously expect to please Him only through and after our works, then it is all pure deception, outwardly honoring God, but inwardly setting up self as a false god. . . .[121]

Here Luther argues that when we fail to believe that God accepts us fully in Christ, and look to some other way to justify or prove ourselves, we commit idolatry. Secular people may look for "favor, grace, and goodwill" in the acquisition of power, or the experience of pleasure, while religious people may trust in their moral virtue or acts of devotion or ministry. But all are fundamentally the same inner transaction. In each case the heart is given to a counterfeit god.

When Paul walked around Athens, he saw that the "city was full of idols" (Acts 17:16). He was speaking of actual physical objects, but once we grasp the biblical definition of idolatry, we realize that every city and indeed every human heart is filled with idols. They are literally everywhere.

Idols are not only pervasive, they are powerful. Why do the Ten Commandments begin with a prohibition of idolatry? It is, Luther argued, because we never break the other commandments without breaking the first. For example, suppose you know that complete transparency in a business negotiation will yield you considerably less leverage than will a small measure of deceit. In that situation, if you lie or obscure inconvenient facts, it is because you have counted success as more important than obedience to God or the good of your "neighbor" with whom you are negotiating. So beneath the sin of lying is the deeper, conditioning sin of idolatry. It could be argued that everything we do wrong—every cruel action, dishonest word, broken promise, self-centered attitude—stems from a conviction deep in our souls that there is something more crucial to our happiness and meaning than the love of God.

Idolatry has power over our actions because it has power over our hearts. Twenty-two-year-old Andrew is out of work and broke because he's terrified that if he takes a job loading boxes in a warehouse he will be stunted for life—earning minimum wage, doing work that only people beneath him do, losing his status among his friends as a cool guy, and perhaps even losing his girlfriend. He had wanted to play baseball, and he nurses that hope, thinking if he could get back into college by playing baseball, then his life would be set. When we set our hope on an idol in this way, we are saying to ourselves, "If I had that, it would fix everything; then I'd feel my life really had value." Now, if anything is our "salvation" we *must* have it, and so we treat it as nonnegotiable. If circumstances threaten to take it away, we are paralyzed with uncontrollable fear; if something or someone has taken it away, we burn with anger and struggle with a sense of despair.

Cultural and Corporate Idols

Thus far we have been speaking of individual idols that distort our personal lives. We know that people develop "fatal attractions" for status and power, for approval and achievement, for romance and sexual pleasure, or for affluence and comfort. Personal idols profoundly drive and shape our behavior, including our work. Idols of comfort and pleasure can make it impossible for a person to work as hard as is necessary to have a faithful and fruitful career. Idols of power and approval, on the other hand, can lead us to overwork or to be ruthless and unbalanced in our work practices. Idols of control take several forms—including intense worry, lack of trust, and micromanagement. While we are usually blind to our own idols, it is not very hard to see them in others, and to see how others' counterfeit gods fill them with anxiety, anger, and discouragement. So the concept of individual idols is not too hard for us to grasp.

However, idols are not only the basis for personal sins and problems; they are also the basis for collective ones. When an individual makes and serves an idol, it creates psychological distortion and trouble; when a family, group, or country makes and serves an idol, it creates social and cultural trouble.[122] To understand this concept of cultural or "corporate" idols (in the sense of a group of people, not in the sense of a business structure), we must begin with a more precise description of culture than we used in Chapter 3. Columbia University professor Andrew Delbanco writes:

> I will use the word culture to mean the stories and symbols by which we try to hold back the melancholy suspicion that we live in a world without meaning. . . . Any history of hope in America must, therefore, make room at its center for this dogged companion of hope—the lurking suspicion that all our getting and spending amounts to nothing more than fidgeting while we wait for death.
>
> All cultures have this need for contact with what William James called the "Ideal Power" through which that "feeling of being in a wider life than that of this world's little interests" may be reached. . . .[123]

Every culture has a set of answers to the questions addressed in the book of Ecclesiastes—questions such as "What are we here to accomplish in our life? What are we getting, spending, and living for?" Without some answers to these big questions, it is impossible to live and make decisions, and every culture is at some level based on a set of shared beliefs about how to answer these questions. So while each individual needs to live for something, so does each society. Or, put another way, every society puts before its members some ideas or values that it says will give life meaning.

Friedrich Nietzsche concurred that every society offers up "ideals" to its members.[124] Ancient cultures called people to live for God (or the gods), for family and tribe or nation. Modern societies turned away from the authorities of religion and tradition, and replaced them with the authorities of reason and individual freedom. Nietzsche was looking mainly at modern cultures, but he observed that all cultures—even self-styled "secular" ones—promote moral absolutes and transcendent values to which (they said) all people must conform if they are to have worth or meaning. These cultural ideals are truly idols in the biblical sense; they are not commended as simply good ideas. Rather, they are treated as holy and unassailable, and promoted with religious fervor and passion. They are said to bestow happiness and fulfillment (earthly forms of salvation). All people are obliged to serve these ideals, and those who despise them are themselves to be rejected. So while ancient cultures ostracized anyone who disbelieved in the gods, modern culture castigates anyone who is thought guilty of bigotry or appears to be an enemy of equality and individual freedom.[125]

If every culture has its idols, how do they influence how we do our work? Keeping in mind that an idol is a good thing turned into an ultimate thing, then a corporate idol is an overemphasis and absolutizing of an admirable cultural trait. We should expect, then, that each culture's emphases have some beneficial influences on work and yet at the same time harmfully distort it. Christians seeking to work faithfully and well must discern the shape of the idols functioning in their professions and industries so as to both affirm the beneficial aspects and offset the excesses and distortions.

So what kinds of corporate and cultural idols are there? Keeping in mind the inevitability of overgeneralization in such a brief treatment, I will provide an overview of the prevailing idols of the three dominant cultures of Western history: traditional, modern, and postmodern. In nearly every field of work, you will encounter a mixture of these sets of cultural idols, because they will have influenced the founders, heroes, leaders, and innovators of the dominant institutions in diverse ways over the course of generations.

Idols of Traditional Cultures

As we just mentioned, traditional cultures in the past and present understand the world to contain moral absolutes that are known mainly through tradition and religion. Wisdom is passed down from one generation to the next through figures of authority such as parents, priests, and rulers. Such cultures teach their members that their lives have meaning if they assume and are faithful to their duties and roles within the community—as sons and daughters, as fathers and mothers, and as members of their tribe and nation. In such cultures, family, race, and nation can become dangerously paramount.

This is the basis for honor killings in such cultures, where some members of a family kill a member perceived to bring dishonor on the clan. This elevation of family in traditional cultures often results in minimal support and recourse to the victims of spousal and child abuse. This also helps us understand why Japanese soldiers in World War II despised Allied prisoners of war who, they reasoned, had put their own individual lives ahead of the nation by not fighting to the death. All of these practices seem almost impossible to understand for those of us in contemporary Western societies.

Nonetheless, in Western societies we have still struggled mightily with the idols of race and racism. American theologian Reinhold Niebuhr understood that the tendency to privilege the interests of one's own tribe or nation over others is due to the "cosmic insecurity" of our sinful hearts.[126] This insecurity fixes on race to bolster our sense of value. We see differences between our own culture and those of others in highly moralistic terms; we look down on other races so we can think of ourselves as superior. This idol can easily grow into something very cruel. As a result, it is possible to make national security or cultural and racial purity into an end in itself, justifying militarism and domestic oppression or at least indifference to the plight of minorities.

The idolatries of more traditional places and cultures also affect our work. The idol of race can mean that many businesses are closed to people and ideas from culturally and racially different backgrounds—to the overall detriment of the company's competitiveness and the community's health. The idol of nationalism, of course, has led industrialists to support militaristic programs that may have seemed patriotic at the time, but in hindsight ruined their reputation for all time.

Traditional cultures make idols out of social stability and the good of the whole over the rights of the individual. This has a major impact on business practices. In Japan, still largely a traditional culture, it has not been acceptable either for workers to move from company to company in order to find a better salary, or for companies to lay workers off to sustain profits. Until the turn of this century, the Japanese ideal had been lifelong employment—employees were expected to stay with the same company their entire lives. In a traditional culture, the profit motive of business is accompanied by a strong social obligation to provide jobs for people. Employees are less concerned with their own pay than with the status and reputation of the company where they are employed.

There are certainly some benefits to this emphasis on loyalty and social stability. However, it can also lead to exploitation of workers, who are often stigmatized if they make (what Western cultures would see as) just demands for increased salary and benefits. It also can lead to economic devastation during economic downturns. A *New York Times* article during the 1992 recession, "No Layoff Ideal Costs Japan Dearly," explained how during downturns U.S. companies are able to more quickly recover financial health—and therefore provide jobs for more people in the long run—by reducing staff. The Japanese ideal led to many companies completely collapsing and doing even more damage to people's lives because their culture did not feel free to make the hard call of layoffs.[127]

Idols of Modern Cultures

Great changes occurred in Western societies approximately five hundred years ago. With the rise of modern science and the philosophical movement called the Enlightenment, modern society dethroned the idols of religion, tribe, and tradition—replacing them with reason, empiricism, and individual freedom as the ultimate values that overrule all others.

The modern value of "reason" includes several elements. One is the ideal of progress, embodied in the unstoppable forward march of science and technology. Modern societies adopted "the conviction that the diffusion of science and technology would bring happier days and that history and politics must be shaped by [this] ideal."[128] It was said that science alone has a rigorous, empirical method that results in proof, not merely speculation or feeling. Also in the modern worldview, absolutely everything has a natural and therefore physical cause. At the popular level this view still has enormous cultural authority. Most people do not venture to make a case in the public square without relying on "scientific evidence," which is seen as objective and unassailable. The implicit idea is that science, given enough time, will be able to answer all questions and solve all problems.[129] Scientific methods have extended beyond the physical and social sciences into the realms of marketing, politics, entertainment. Modern culture stopped looking to the wisdom of the ancients or to any revelation from religious authorities except for optional, private "spiritual" comfort. To build a flourishing society, we need only human reason informed by the scientific method.

Closely related to this radical new hope in human reason was the absolutizing of individual freedom. Modern societies no longer saw the world as containing binding moral norms of truth to which all people must submit. Rather, they insisted that there was no standard higher than the right of the individual to choose the life he or she wanted to live. The only moral wrong, in this view, was to keep other individuals from choosing to live as they found fulfilling. That meant that, ultimately, there was no moral authority or cause higher than the happiness of the self.[130] As many have pointed out, this made "choice" and feelings into something sacred and holy. In the modern world, "now, the individual was the center of the universe, and the creature beyond all else entitled to absolute respect."[131] In other words, the human self had replaced God.

The idols of modern culture have had a profound influence on the shape of our work today. In traditional societies people found their meaning and sense of value by submitting their interests and sacrificing their desires to serve higher causes like God, family, and other people. In modern societies there is often no higher cause than individual interests and desires. This shift powerfully changed the role of work in people's lives—it now became the way we defined ourselves. Traditional cultures tended to see people's place on the social ladder as assigned by nature or convention, each family having its "proper place." That view had put too little stock in the role of individual talent, ambition, and hard work for determining the outcome of one's life. But modern society responded by putting too much stock in the autonomous person. Philosopher Luc Ferry explains how the new individualism of modern society influenced our work:

> In the aristocratic [traditional] world-view, work was considered a defect, a servile activity—literally, reserved for slaves. In the modern world-view, it becomes an arena for self-realization, a means not only of educating oneself but also of fulfillment. . . . Work becomes the defining activity of man. . . . His aim is to create himself by remaking the world. . . .[132]

So the modern idol of individualism has tended to raise work from being a good thing to being nearly a form of salvation. At the same time, the modern idols of reason and empiricism intensified the work experience by creating a pressure for higher production than had ever been applied before. Near the end of the nineteenth century, Frederick Taylor developed "Scientific Management," which was called the "rationalization" of production.[133] It was the intense application of scientific methods to business processes to generate maximum efficiency.

At the time, laborers in the factories taken over by Taylor's methods reacted with fury. They felt dehumanized—since all personal discretion and initiative was taken out of their hands—and driven like slaves. Taylor's system valued every task being simplified, standardized, and executed with absolute uniformity every time. As many have pointed out, this is how machines work. Peter Drucker, the foremost critic of Taylor's approach argued that the extreme rationalization of work did indeed treat human beings like cogs in a mechanism. "Machines," he wrote, "work best if they do only one task, if they do it repetitively, and if they do the simplest possible task. . . . [But] the human being . . . is a very poorly designed machine tool. The human being excels . . . in coordination. He excels in relating perception to action. He works best if the entire human being, muscles, senses, and mind is engaged in the work."[134]

Is the influence of modern idols positive for our work today? The answer is somewhat yes but ultimately no. Modern idols bestowed greater dignity on some kinds of work than had existed in ancient cultures, and in this sense it came closer to the high regard the Bible has for labor, but it overshot the mark in many ways. We are far more efficient and productive than we used to be, but this progress has come at a great cost. My own grandfather's experience was a good case study of the mixture of good and evil brought to the realm of work in the modern age. Born in Italy in 1880 into a traditional culture and a family of potters, he told his father that he didn't want to follow in his career footsteps. He was told that it would be impossible in that stratified society to get another job or even move to another village. In response he emigrated to America in 1897, a far more modern society allowing a social mobility unthinkable in his homeland. There he began to work on the subways under New York City under grueling conditions that demanded high productivity but provided no safety, a situation that would not have happened to him in his own village. After almost losing a leg in a work accident he moved to Wilmington, Delaware, where through his ability to start his own butcher shop—which also would have been unlikely in his own village—he established himself in his new country. Within his lifetime he was liberated, dashed, and rehabilitated by the effects of modern culture.

Idols of Postmodern Cultures

Beginning with the writings of the philosopher Friedrich Nietzsche in the latter half of the nineteenth century, a new cultural shift began to occur in Western societies.[135] Long before the horrors of the world wars, Nietzsche declared that the idea that science will lead to inevitable human progress was an idol—a new quasi-religious faith—and that it had no grounding in reality. Science can tell us only what *is*, never how things *ought* to be. Human beings are capable of kindness and unselfishness but also of cruelty and violence, and science will simply serve the interests of whoever is in power. There is no particular reason, he pointed out, to think science will somehow lead us to a better world. It could just as easily lead us into a bleak future through armed conflict, or an ecological disaster, or the rise of tyrants who use technology for powerful social control.

Nietzsche struck a blow not only to the modern idol of reason and science, but also to the new modern morality of individual rights and freedom. With great force, he pointed out the deep inconsistency of the modern view. Modern culture tells us there are no moral absolutes and everyone must choose his or her own standard for right and wrong, yet it then turns and says we must respect human rights and honor the freedom and dignity of every human being. "But on what basis?" Nietzsche would ask. If there are no moral absolutes, then how can you arbitrarily declare that there are? If human beings are simply the product of the same natural processes that formed rust and rocks, why does every person deserve to be treated with equality and dignity?

Though Nietzsche's arguments were deeply disturbing, his basic points were very telling, and in so many ways the disasters and atrocities of the twentieth century only seemed to bear them out. As a result, despite the fact that in Western society there is still a strong latent influence from traditional worldviews such as Christianity, along with much of the older modern optimism about science, progress, and human freedom, there has been a pervasive shift called the "postmodern turn." It is more a mood than a coherent set of beliefs. There is far more cynicism about all truth claims and plans for society—both older traditional ones and more modern, liberal ones. Movies and novels about the future in the mid-twentieth century often depicted a human society filled with unceasing progress in health, education, scientific knowledge, and social harmony. Today nearly all movies and novels are far more pessimistic and narrate all sorts of dystopian outcomes.

Despite Nietzsche's program to rid the culture of idols, many have pointed out that ultimately postmodern thought makes an idol out of reality as it is. Writers such as Edward Docx, in his article "Postmodernism Is Dead," lays out this criticism well. He points out that if all moral claims are really just power plays and the product of one's social and cultural location, as postmodern theorists argue, then it becomes impossible to critique any condition in a society. No one has any ability to mount a program of reform or denounce injustice. Postmodernism enshrines the present reality, then, as an absolute.[136]

The most prominent critic of Nietzsche and the results of postmodernism was the German philosopher Martin Heidegger. He identified the idol of our culture today when he called us "the world of technology." Luc Ferry explains Heidegger's point:

> Before all else, technique concerns means and not ends. . . . Instead of being inspired by transcendental ideas . . . the modern economy functions like Darwinian natural selection. . . . No one [today] can be reasonably convinced that this teeming and disruptive evolutionary impulse . . . leads infallibly to what is better. . . . For the first time in the history of life, a living species holds the means to destroy the entire planet, and this species does not know where it is going.[137]

Heidegger, Docx, and others such as Jacques Ellul[138] are saying that technology, uncertainty, and the market have become the idols of a postmodern society. Because in postmodern society no one is sure or can agree about "ends" or goals for the human race, we now have only "means" or techniques. Since there is no longer any dominant vision of healthy human life or good human society, we are left with nothing but individual competition for personal success and power. If something *can* be done through technology, it *will* be done, because our technology has no higher ideals or moral values to guide it or limit it.

The resulting fragmentation of society caused by the postmodern turn is itself a pervasive topic of debate in the academy. Both Robert Bellah and Andrew Delbanco argue the case that any cohesive society needs to give individuals something bigger and greater than themselves to live for. Delbanco argues that, ironically, the heyday of the new Left in the 1960s and of the new Right in the 1980s "cooperated in installing instant gratification as the hallmark of the good life. . . . What was lost . . . was any conception of a common destiny worth tears, sacrifice, and maybe even death."[139]

Delbanco agrees with others who say that in the end, postmodern idols cause individuals to become dupes of advertisers—falling into "unconscious conformity with other interchangeable products of the marketplace."[140] Many writers argue convincingly that the values of the market—consumerism and cost-benefit efficiencies—are now spreading into every part of life, even family life. This is because modern capitalism is no longer simply a useful instrument for the distribution of goods and services, but has become a near-absolute idol.[141] And even in the most successful capitalist societies like that of the United States, many recognize the cultural contradiction that consumerism tends to undermine the very virtues of self-control and responsibility on which capitalism is founded.[142]

How does this shifting of mood and meaning affect our work now? I spoke to a man, now in his eighties, who was one of the pioneers of the hedge fund industry. He told me that in the late 1950s and most of the 1960s, the great majority of the best and the brightest did not want to go into financial services—they wanted to go into education and science. They wanted to teach the young, put people on the moon, and solve world hunger. And the leading voices of the day told them they could do it. At some point by the late 1980s he sensed a change in society. There was far less optimism about social progress or even how to define it. People were divided by the culture wars. Cynicism set in, and over time the most ambitious and talented people wanted to go into business and finance. The perception was that unless you were a highly paid professional, you could not live a fulfilled, free life. "It's not healthy," he told me, and he was right. He was agreeing with the analyses of the philosophers and scholars, but rather than observing an ideological trend, he saw how the shift played out concretely in young adults' career choices. He was old enough to see the shift from a largely modern to a more postmodern understanding of work.

The most obvious effect of the postmodern "means-without-an-end" idolatry (at the time of this writing) is the widespread deception, fraud, and self-interested actions of financial companies, revealed in the recession of 2008 and its aftermath. Naomi Wolf, writing in the British daily newspaper *The Guardian*, reviewed what could be seen just in the newspaper headlines of June and July 2012. She goes down the list: Barclays Bank and others colluding to manipulate interest rates; the HSBC banking group fined one billion dollars for not preventing money laundering ("a highly profitable activity not to prevent") between 2004 and 2010; 215 million dollars of customer money "missing" at Peregrine Capital, whose founder faces criminal charges after a suicide attempt; Wells Fargo agreeing to pay 175 million dollars in fines for ("again, very lucratively") automatically charging African American and Hispanic mortgagees costlier rates on their subprime mortgages than white people with identical credit ratings. Bank of America and SunTrust were also fined for the same practice. The 2008 recession itself, of course, was triggered by bankers profiting from the sales of enormous numbers of mortgages that were packaged in ways that concealed their low underlying value.

The conclusion of this sad litany is found in the subtitle of Wolf's article: "The media's 'bad apple' thesis no longer works. We're seeing systemic corruption in banking—and systemic collusion."[143]

Those with more politically liberal sensibilities are quick to perceive the postmodern idols of "means without ends" in the area of business. They are not as sensitive to the even more pervasive problem that we now get a sense of self not from our roles in family and society, but as consumers. We are encouraged to create a persona through the brands we choose to purchase and the identity we are able to construct for ourselves online.

This phenomenon has an especially profound impact on the fields of media, entertainment, and marketing. I have spoken to many of my church members in marketing and advertising about the shift away from advertising the benefits of *products* in favor of advertising a life story that promises the consumer an enhanced *identity* and a higher quality of life. Yale philosopher Nicholas Wolterstorff observes that modern culture defines the happy life as a life that is "going well"—full of experiential pleasure—while to the ancients, the happy life meant the life that is lived well, with character, courage, humility, love, and justice.[144] So all who work in marketing and promotion will be expected to promise people not merely that their products will work satisfactorily, but also that they will bring them happiness.

I spoke to a man and woman who both were advertising executives and were thinking of leaving their respective companies. The woman's firm had just two major clients, and both were cosmetics companies. "The message they want me to send about our products—that this will help you finally find love and love yourself—is toxic." The man worked for an agency with a sports car company for a client. He was under pressure, not for the first time, to market his car as a means to sex appeal. Both workers pushed back and got strong resistance in return. The man kept his job because he changed the message from "sex appeal" to "high-performance vehicle" and did it so skillfully and compellingly that the client and his company were satisfied. The woman, however, did not succeed and had to leave her firm, going into business for herself.

Christians agree that when we sell and market, we need to show potential customers that a product "adds value" to their lives. That doesn't mean it can *give* them a life. But because Christians have a deeper understanding of human well-being, we will often find ourselves swimming against the very strong currents of the corporate idols of our culture.

Finding Hope for Our Work

We have been describing what work was designed to be and what has gone wrong with it. Even if we find ourselves doing the kind of work we want and in the best sorts of work environments, the broken nature of work seems overwhelming. "What hope is there for work? How can we put work right?" we may ask. How do we look past the deep problems and realize God's purpose and plan? Is that a realistic goal, or is it just a nice idea that has no bearing on tomorrow's meeting or next year's career change?

We can begin to answer these questions only by first settling one sure fact: Nothing will be put perfectly right, as St. Paul says, until the "day of Christ" at the end of history (Philippians 1:6; 3:12). Until then all creation "groans" (Romans 8:22) and is subject to decay and weakness. So work will be put *completely*

right only when heaven is reunited with earth and we find ourselves in our "true country." To talk about fully redeeming work
is sometimes naïvete, sometimes hubris.

Yet all is not lost. The transcendent hope depicted so poi-
gnantly in "Leaf by Niggle," and the ecstatic vision of what creative endeavor will then be like, can go a long way to helping us
work with satisfaction within the limits of this world. The Christian gospel decidedly furnishes us with the resources for more
inspired, realistic, satisfying, and faithful work today. How?

First, the gospel provides an alternate story line for our work;
this is vital because all work is propelled by a worldview or a narrative account of what human life is all about and what will help
us thrive.

Second, the Christian faith gives us a new and rich conception
of work as partnering with God in his love and care for the world.
This biblical conception helps us appreciate *all* work, from the
most simple to the most complex, by both believers and nonbelievers. So Christians who grasp a biblical theology of work learn
not only to value and participate in the work of all people but to
also see ways to work distinctively as Christians.

Third, the gospel gives us a particularly sensitive new moral
compass, through a host of sound ethical guidelines to help us
make decisions, as well as wise counsel about human hearts.

Finally, the gospel radically changes our motives for work and
fills us with a new and durable inner power that will be with us
through thick and thin.[145]

Most books and programs that help people integrate their
faith with their work tend to focus on only one or two of these
factors. Some, for example, emphasize the first. They take a
somewhat academic tack and constitute theological principles

into a "Christian approach" to art, government, economics, and so on. Some concentrate almost completely on the second. They fear that an overemphasis on a biblical worldview in work leads to triumphalism and fails to appreciate God's broad providential activity. Others take a more personal and experiential approach, inviting people to encounter Christ in a new way and emphasizing the inner power that comes from a gospel-transformed heart. Still others fear that focus on inner-heart transformation puts all the weight on personal peace and success and ignores the social-justice implications of the gospel, in which Christians are responsible to serve others through their work.

But all of these emphases and concerns are correct—and in the final part of the book, we seek to show that they are ultimately complementary and very practical. Indeed one of the reasons the Bible's view of work is so compelling and so helpful in all cultures, social settings, and vocations is because it is so rich and multidimensional.

PART THREE

The Gospel and Work

NINE

A New Story for Work

*So whether you eat or drink or whatever you do, do it all
for the glory of God.*

1 Corinthians 10:31

Making Sense of the World

People cannot make sense of anything without attaching it to a
story line. After the attacks of September 11, 2001, no one mentioned the event without placing it into some kind of narrative
structure. Some said, "This is the result of America's abuse of its
imperial power in the world." Others said, "There are many evil
people out there who hate us because we are a good and free
country." Depending on which story you believed, you would be
associated with the antagonists or the protagonists, and your
response—both emotions and actions—would be completely
different.

A classic illustration of the need for stories comes from philosopher Alasdair MacIntyre in his book *After Virtue*. He asks
that you imagine you are standing at a bus stop when a young
man you do not know comes up to you and says, "The name of

the common wild duck is *Histrionicus histrionicus histrionicus.*"
Even though you understand the sentence, his action makes no
sense. What does it mean? The only way to make sense of it is to
try to learn the story into which this event fits. Perhaps the young
man is mentally ill; that would explain it. Or what if yesterday
someone of your gender, age, height, and general appearance
had approached the young man in the library, asking him the
Latin word for the wild duck, and today he had mistaken you for
that person? That would explain it too. Or perhaps the young
man is a foreign spy "waiting at a prearranged rendezvous and
uttering the ill-chosen code sentence which will identify him to
his contact." The first story is sad, the second is comic, and the
third is dramatic. But the point is, without a handle on the story,
there's no way to understand the meaning of what happened and
no way to know how to answer the man.[146]

If you call the police when it was a simple case of mistaken
identity, it will be very embarrassing. If you pick a fight with
someone who is a trained assassin, the result will be even worse!
But in any case, if you get the story wrong, your response will be
wrong. And if you get the story of the world wrong—if, for example, you see life here as mainly about self-actualization and
self-fulfillment rather than the love of God—you will get your
life responses wrong, including the way you go about your work.

Stories and Worldviews

What are the elements of a story? While there are many good
scholarly analyses of narrative structure, here is a simple way to put
it.[147] A story begins when something knocks life off balance. Then
the story progresses, or the plot "thickens," as the protagonists

struggle to restore that balance and peace while antagonistic forces block and resist them. Finally, the story ends as the struggle results in either the restoration of balance or the failure to recover it.

So for a story to be a story, there must be a problem that makes life not as it ought to be. If we say, "Little Red Riding Hood took some food to her grandmother and they ate it together," we might have a charming description, but it is hardly a story, since it has no plot.[148] A story must also have some concept and possibility of things being put right. "Little Red Riding Hood was at her grandmother's house, but a wolf broke in and ate them both"—a more dramatic set of facts, but again, it's not a story. So a story must have an account of how life should be, an explanation of how it got thrown off balance, and some proposed solution as to what will put life right again.

Now, the significance of stories is this. While many stories are often no more than entertainment, narratives are actually so foundational to how we think that they determine how we understand and live life itself. The term "worldview," from the German word *Weltanschauung,* means the comprehensive perspective from which we interpret all of reality. But a worldview is not merely a set of philosophical bullet points. It is essentially a master narrative, a fundamental story about (a) what human life in the world should be like, (b) what has knocked it off balance, and (c) what can be done to make it right.[149] No one can really function in the world without some working answers to those big questions, and so, to provide those answers, we adopt a world-story, a narrative that explains things—a worldview.

Everyone knows that things in this world are seriously out of whack. No one claims that his or her own life is as it should be, let alone the whole world. There is something wrong *within* us.

Nothing ever seems to make us happy or fulfilled except in the most fleeting way. There is also wrong *among* us. The world is filled with poverty, war, suffering, and injustice. Something seems to have knocked the whole world off balance. But what is it? Who deserves the blame? And what is the solution? As soon as you begin to answer these questions, you arrive at a story that you will begin to live out. We are wired to move through our lives chasing and rehearsing narratives that will promise to bring the world back into balance.

MacIntyre argues that human actions are "enacted narrative." All people are living out some mental world-story that gives their lives meaning.[150] That story may be about the struggle of a just cause like saving the environment, or your personal quest to find true love or to be successful despite adverse social origins and expectations. Or perhaps the story is one of freedom and equality, in which you are bringing a family from an oppressive situation into a new country and new life. Maybe the drama is one in which you forge your own unique sexual, cultural, or political identity against the prejudices of others. In each case you are putting yourself into a larger story that assumes the world would be a better place if more people were doing what you were doing. You may believe the world would be dramatically improved if everyone were free-spirited and progressive and willing to defy oppressive traditions. Or perhaps you think the world would be far better off if we were standing for proven moral absolutes. In each case, the person assumes he or she is a protagonist, one of the good people contributing to the way the world ought to be.

Worldviews, however, are not private or unique. In fact, whole groups and cultures have their own preferred world-story with generally accepted answers to the big questions and shared idols that heighten the drama. Leslie Stevenson's classic book, *Seven Theories of Human Nature*, lists influential views of human nature pioneered by prominent thinkers who influenced whole societies. Plato saw our main problem as being the physical body and its weakness; for Marx it was unjust economic systems; for Freud it was inner unconscious conflicts between desire and conscience; for Sartre it was not realizing we are completely free since there are no objective values; for B.F. Skinner it was not realizing we are completely determined by our environment; and for Konrad Lorenz it was our innate aggression because of our evolutionary past.[151] Each of these theories is really a story—of what is wrong with us and what we can do about it. And each of these views of reality has been enormously powerful, influencing societies and fields of inquiry and work. When any one of these worldviews grips the imagination of a culture, it has a profound influence on how life is lived, even for those who do not accept that worldview.

One of the main places that we personally live out the drama of our personal and social narratives is in our daily work. Our worldview places our work in the context of a history, a cause, a quest, and a set of protagonists and antagonists, and in so doing it frames the strategy of our work at a high level. At a day-to-day level, our worldview will shape our individual interactions and decisions.

As we read in the foreword, Katherine Alsdorf was given a new story—the gospel—that was different from the dominant story of Silicon Valley, which evangelized fervently and optimistically about the power of technology to change the world for the better. The advertising executives we mentioned in the last chapter worked amid a story in which self-expression, sexual pleasure, and affluence were the meaning of life, and survival of the fittest was just the way life works. The gospel, however, teaches that the meaning of life is to love God and love our neighbor, and that the operating principle is servanthood. These contrasts may sound at first rather high and abstract, but they became very practical when these two executives crafted messages in their advertising.

The Gospel and Other Worldviews

We have said that any worldview consists of posing and answering three questions:

1. How are things supposed to be?
2. What is the main problem with things as they are?
3. What is the solution and how can it be realized?

Stevenson's book on human nature includes Christianity among its "theories," but the author points out how different Christianity is from the alternatives. He observes that "If God has made man for fellowship with Himself, and if man has turned away and broken his relationship to God, then only God can forgive man and restore the relationship."[152] In other words, the biblical worldview uniquely understands the nature, problem, and salvation of humankind as fundamentally *relational*. We were made for a relationship with God, we lost our relationship with God through sin against him, and we can be brought back into that relationship through his salvation and grace.

Plato, Marx, and Freud identify some part of the created world as the main problem and some other part of the created world as

the main solution. The protagonists and antagonists of their respective world-stories are played by finite things. Thus, Marxism
assumes that our problems come from greedy capitalists who
won't share the means of economic production with the people.
The solution is a totalitarian state. Freud, on the other hand, believed that our problems come from repression of deep desires for
pleasure. The villains are played by the repressive moral "gatekeepers" in society, like the church. The solution is the unrepressed
freedom of the individual. Many people have a worldview that to
some degree is indebted to the Greeks and Plato. They think the
problem with the world rests in undisciplined, selfish people who
won't submit to traditional moral values and responsibilities. The
solution is a "revival" of religion, morality, and virtue in society.

Philosopher Al Wolters writes:

> The great danger is to always single out some aspect of
> God's good creation and identify *it,* rather than the
> alien intrusion of sin, as the villain. Such an error con-
> ceives of the good-evil dichotomy as intrinsic to the
> creation itself . . . something in the good creation is
> identified as [the source] of evil. In the course of his-
> tory, this "something" has been variously identified
> as . . . the body and its passions (Plato and much of
> Greek philosophy), as culture in distinction from na-
> ture (Rousseau and Romanticism), as authority figures
> in society and family (psychodynamic psychology), as
> economic forces (Marx), as technology and manage-
> ment (Heidegger and existentialists). . . . As far as I
> can tell, the Bible is unique in its rejection of all at-
> tempts to either demonize some part of creation as the

root of our problems or to idolize some part of creation as the solution. All other religions, philosophies, and worldviews in one way or another fall into the trap of [idolatry]—of failing to keep creation and fall distinct. And this trap is an ever-present danger for Christians [as well].[153]

Look again at the uniqueness of Christianity. Only the Christian worldview locates the problem with the world *not* in any part of the world or in any particular group of people but in sin itself (our loss of relationship with God). And it locates the solution in God's grace (our restoration of a relationship with God through the work of Christ). Sin infects us all, and so we cannot simply divide the world into the heroes and the villains. (And if we did, we would certainly have to count ourselves among the latter as well as the former.) Without an understanding of the gospel, we will be either naïvely utopian or cynically disillusioned. We will be demonizing something that isn't bad enough to explain the mess we are in; and we will be idolizing something that isn't powerful enough to get us out of it. This is, in the end, what all other worldviews do.

The Christian story line works beautifully to make sense of things and even to help us appreciate the truth embedded in stories that clearly come from another worldview. The Christian story line, or worldview, is: creation (plan), fall (problem), redemption and restoration (solution):

The whole world is good. God made the world and everything in it was good. There are no intrinsically evil parts of the world. Nothing is evil in its origin. As Tolkien explained about his archvillain in the *Lord of the Rings* trilogy, in the beginning "even Sauron was not so." You can find this "creational good" in anything.

The whole world is fallen. There is no aspect of the world affected by sin more or less than any other. For example, are emotion and passions untrustworthy and reason infallible? Is the physical bad and the spiritual good? Is the day-to-day world profane but religious observances good? None of these are true; but non-Christian story lines must adopt some variations of these in order to villainize and even demonize some created thing instead of sin.

The whole world is going to be redeemed. Jesus is going to redeem spirit and body, reason and emotion, people and nature. There is no part of reality for which there is no hope.

The gospel is the true story that God made a good world that was marred by sin and evil, but through Jesus Christ he redeemed it at infinite cost to himself, so that someday he will return to renew all creation; end all suffering and death; and restore absolute peace, justice, and joy in the world forever. The vast implications of this gospel worldview—about the character of God, the goodness of the material creation, the value of the human person, the fallenness of all people and all things, the primacy of love and grace, the importance of justice and truth, the hope of redemption—affect everything, and especially our work.

Here's an example. Early in his career as a school administrator, our friend Bill Kurtz started to see that this gospel story line— what the world should be, how it had gone wrong, and the hope for the future—gave him a better vision for education in poor inner-city schools. All the individual stories of brokenness—of problems at home, of no sleep and inadequate nutrition, of gangs on the street and drugs in the building—had reinforced a culture of rebellion and hopelessness in the schools. The attitude about school for many of the kids was "why bother." He wanted to bring the hope of the gospel story into his work.

Now in the field of urban education today there are many competing story lines about what education should be, what its main problem is, and what needs to change. As a matter of fact, education itself is often viewed as the savior for the ills of poverty and systemic injustice. Students are the subjects of continuous analysis as one strategy or another is applied to their educational experience. Bill found that the gospel gave him a more comprehensive understanding of the problems facing the schools and a hope for redemption that incorporated some of the best practices of his field but did not idolize them.

His approach has been holistic, with the recognition that the gospel could actually shape the culture of a school community. In 2004 he launched a public charter high school in Denver to serve a very diverse student population. One grade at a time he helped create a culture of shared accountability and success in the school. Every morning students gather, along with their teachers, for morning meeting. Morning meetings provide an opportunity for the community to celebrate success through weekly awards, by giving shout-outs to one another for acts of service and living the school's values, and by sharing stories that point to a story of hope. But the brokenness is addressed as well. To help change behaviors where students fail to live the values of the community, students participate in public apologies where they hold one another accountable and support one another to live the school's core values better. If a student or teacher is late to school, they apologize to the rest of the community. He recognized the students' innate need to be known but held accountable and created en environment where no one could be lost in the cracks. While good teachers have certainly been key, Bill attributes the school's success to its culture and their shared, singular goal to get 100 percent of its seniors into four-year colleges. The school has seen amazing success—every single senior in the school's history has earned a four-year college acceptance. This first school has grown into a network of six top-performing schools across Denver.

The Gospel and Business

The gospel worldview will have all kinds of influence—profound and mundane, strategic and tactical—on how you actually do your work. Every field of work is to some degree influenced by alternate worldviews and their attendant idols, each assigning ultimate value to some idol—that doesn't fully take into consideration our sin or God's grace. The particulars of how the gospel works out in each field are endlessly rich—in fact, hundreds of people meet each month at Redeemer to discuss these very ideas within their respective fields. So, while these ideas deserve book-length treatments in their own right, let me sketch here the outlines of the gospel implications in just a few fields of work.

What are some of the idols of business, for example? Money and power certainly top the list. But remember that an idol is a good thing that we make into an ultimate thing. Corporate profits and influence, stewarded wisely, are a healthy means to a good end: They are vital to creating new products to serve customers, giving an adequate return to investors for the use of their money, and paying employees well for their work. Similarly, individual compensation is an appropriate reward for one's contributions and is necessary to provide for oneself and one's family. But it is not our identity, our salvation, or even our source of security and comfort. The Christian worker or business leader who has experienced God's grace—who knows "You are not your own; you were bought at a price" (1 Corinthians 6:19–20)—is free to honor God, love neighbors, and serve the common good through work. In fact, at Redeemer we believe this idea is so important for life in the city that we work with entrepreneurs and offer classes to help them think through how the story of the gospel shapes their vision for their new venture. Whether it's a for-profit business, a nonprofit, or an arts venture, we point each entrepreneur to a vision of serving a need in a way that reflects God's plan for the world.

We find and share examples of good leaders—Christian and otherwise—who balance the interests of all the company's stakeholders: stockholders, customers, employees, suppliers, and even the surrounding community. Milton Hershey, for example, founded the Hershey Chocolate Company in 1903 with the innovation of putting milk into the chocolate bar. The company prospered, as did all the dairy farmers in the surrounding countryside. When the Depression hit and business fell apart, Hershey committed to not lay off his employees. Instead he created his own public works projects in the town and put the employees to work building houses, an amusement park, and a hotel. Toward the end of his life, he and his wife (who were childless) founded a boarding school for orphans to give them practical life skills within a supportive community. The trust that runs the school owns a large portion of the company stock, so today the school is funded by dividends and stock appreciation.

At one level, this should all seem to go without saying. The idea that businesses should advance the social good has been regaining its proper place in the last decade, helped along by the string of business scandals in recent years. As a case in point, in a 2009 speech James Murdoch, son of News Corp. Chief Executive Rupert Murdoch, told the audience at the Edinburgh Television Festival that the "only reliable and perpetual guarantor of independence is profit." Yet in the wake of the phone-hacking scandal at News Corp.'s UK newspaper unit, his sister Elisabeth Murdoch could say to the same audience three years later that her brother "left something out," declaring "profit without purpose is a recipe for disaster." She went on to say, "Personally, I believe one of the biggest lessons of the past year has been the need for any organization to discuss, affirm and institutionalize a rigorous set of values based on an explicit statement of purpose."[154]

Yet despite this growing consensus, it is probably fair to say that the implicit assumptions in the marketplace are that making money is the main thing in life, that business is fundamentally about accumulating and wielding power, and that maximizing profit within legal limits is an end in itself. The reason is that sin runs through the heart of every worker and the culture of every enterprise. The result is polluted rivers, poor service, unjust compensation, entitlement attitudes, dead-end jobs, dehumanizing bureaucracy, backstabbing, and power grabs. This is why it is so important for us to be intentional in applying the counter-narrative of the gospel to business.

While from the outside there might not be immediately noticeable differences between a well-run company reflecting a gospel worldview and one reflecting primarily the world-story of the marketplace, inside the differences could be very noticeable. The gospel-centered business would have a discernible vision for serving the customer in some unique way, a lack of adversarial relationships and exploitation, an extremely strong emphasis on excellence and product quality, and an ethical environment that goes "all the way down" to the bottom of the organizational chart and to the realities of daily behavior, even when high ethics mean a loss of margin. In the business animated by the gospel worldview, profit is simply one of many important bottom lines.

My friend Don Flow has overlaid the story line of the gospel on the prevalent worldview of the automotive dealership business. The typical narrative in an auto dealership is to sell each car for the highest price you can, and so sales people are rewarded for identifying and wooing the highest paying customers. Don's vision emphasized the value of a good automobile to each and every customer. But he discovered a problem: Women and minorities were paying more for their cars than more negotiation-savvy white males. He decided to set a flat-rate on all cars—no negotiating—to effect equal opportunity pricing.

Now, Don was the owner of his company and had the authority to make major changes. Most people do not have this freedom. Yet one of the things less senior employees can do is ask questions about the company's mission and, if it is a sound one, treat it seriously and help keep it in the conversation. Leaders often feel overwhelmed by the cynicism and apathy of their employees and lose their drive to hold true to the company's values. Your care and commitment to those values, assuming they are good ones, could be just the encouragement your boss needs.

To be a Christian in business, then, means much more than just being honest or not sleeping with your coworkers. It even means more than personal evangelism or holding a Bible study at the office. Rather, it means thinking out the implications of the gospel worldview and God's purposes for your whole work life—and for the whole of the organization under your influence.

The Gospel and Journalism

We must think out the Christian worldview's implications in every field, and often those implications are subtle. For example, does the gospel have an impact on how you do journalism? You could say, "No, I just report facts objectively." But there is no "view from nowhere." Even the choice of what is reported on as news reflects someone's values and beliefs about what is important. This is why we can readily identify the editorial strategy, or bias, of every journalistic outlet: This one is progressive, while that one is conservative; this one idolizes innovation, while that one idolizes wealth; and this other one idolizes self-determination. Furthermore, if success is too important to a journalist—if it functions as an idol in his or her life—then that goal will color the filter of what they decide to report on and how they write about it.

It is impossible to do a story without heroes and villains. The best journalists do a good job of reporting empirical facts as objectively as possible. But the facts you play up and the ones you play down or leave out, and how you relate them to one another—all this is done in the service of a background narrative filled with assumptions about which forces in the world are good and which are bad. It is seldom difficult, if you pay attention, to see that narrative at work in how the story is presented. Some have argued convincingly that the field of journalism, like many vocational fields, has a "religious" character to it, with sets of doctrines and folkways that are enforced by a kind of priesthood.[155]

What might Christian journalists do differently? I would argue that the gospel worldview—which does not idolize or demonize anything in creation—can uniquely equip a journalist to be even-handed and open-minded in his or her reporting and writing. As we observed above, every other worldview tends to put too much faith in some things and too little in others. So whatever the basic worldview of a journalist, it will lead to being more naïvely positive or unnecessarily cynical and skeptical than if they held the gospel worldview.

Let me offer a simple example. In most stories of crisis our modern, cause-and-effect worldview very quickly seeks someone or something to blame. After Hurricane Katrina hit New Orleans there was a finite period of time in which the basic news of devastation was reported. Very quickly, the story devolved into attempts to cast blame: on the builders of the sea wall or the federal government and its slow response. Not to say that flaws in city planning or unresponsive government agencies aren't problems worthy of reporting, but the need to blame some aspect of creation is a human impulse—not a gospel one. The gospel tells us the fall results in brokenness in nature and in people. The real "story" of the gospel is the evidence of redemption and renewal. The stories of sacrifice and perseverance are a more fitting culmination of the gospel narrative than stories of neglect.

The Gospel and Higher Education

Andrew Delbanco's fine book *College: What It Was, Is, and Should Be* explains how changes in our culture's dominant worldviews have led to crises in the area of higher education. He notes that older worldviews (both Christian and Greco-Roman) believed that much important wisdom had to be rediscovered afresh by new generations as they wrestled with older texts about how to understand and live well in the world. Today we are more influenced heavily by the Enlightenment view, which saw only empirical and scientific knowledge as true in the highest sense. "This way of evaluating the worth of knowledge . . . poses a severe challenge to the humanities—at least to the extent that humanists remain concerned with preserving truth by rearticulating it rather than advancing truth by discarding the old in favor of the new."[156] C.S. Lewis put the same idea like this:

> For the wise men of old the cardinal problem had been how to conform the soul to reality, and the solution had been knowledge, self-discipline, and virtue. For . . . applied science . . . the problem is how to subdue reality to the wishes of men; the solution is a technique.[157]

Delbanco shows how this change in worldview is having a direct negative impact on the study of humanities in Western societies, which he argues is crucial to developing people capable of "reflective citizenship." Elsewhere in his book he laments how a college education is becoming increasingly inaccessible to those without means. The intense competition for a relatively small number of openings in the great universities of our country means that only those very well prepared, tutored, counseled, and financed can get in. Students from poorer communities cannot hope to get the same kind of support. Increasingly, the best education enables the elite classes to simply perpetuate themselves and leave the rest of the population behind. Not only are there fewer poor students getting into elite schools, there is a widening gap between top academic institutions and much of the middle class, who see these institutions as arrogant and out of touch with the values and experience of ordinary people. Underlying all these trends is the modern idea of meritocracy—the belief that those who get into the good schools deserve to be there because they are the best and the brightest. In a *New York Times* op-ed piece, "A Smug Education?" Delbanco points out that there is some truth to the charge that when students make it into the most selective universities, they are taught that others who could not get in are beneath them, which breeds "smugness and self-satisfaction."

Remarkably, the Columbia professor points out that the original founders of Ivy League schools were "stringent Protestants" who believed "the mark of salvation was not high self-esteem but humbling awareness of one's lowliness in the eyes of God. . . . Those whom God favors are granted grace not for any worthiness of their own, but by God's unmerited mercy."[158] Delbanco is not himself a Christian, and he hopes that our secular culture can come up with some basis upon which to humble our elites, but he is clear-eyed in his recognition that the Christian worldview has the resources to keep the egos of the successful and wealthy in check, which is an enormous boost to social cohesion. But today the Christian idea—that no one deserves a good life, that all wealth and talent and power are only a gift of God—has largely been lost in our culture, and the "dark side of our meritocracy" is now creating greater inequities than existed before.

This is all highly suggestive for Christian educators and any others who work in the realm of ideas. In future decades, it may be that

Catholic and Protestant colleges will be in the forefront of the preservation and recovery of the humanities—as the monasteries saved the works of ancient literature during the Middle Ages. Christian educators should be motivated by the gospel to find ways to resist the enormous economic pressures that are today working against both the quality and accessibility of higher education.

The Gospel and the Arts

The art world also has its idols, to be sure. As in any field, some artists will make financial profit the ultimate value and do their work accordingly. And, in general, those who play to the crowd, as it were, produce work that is highly sentimental and saccharine, or filled with shock value, gratuitous sex, and violence. Many artists disdain colleagues who make art for profit; instead they uphold self-expression, originality, and freedom as the ultimate values controlling the work they do. But their self-righteous attitudes betray the fact that there are deep worldviews in play—each with its own sets of demons, idols, heroes, orthodoxies, and redemptive pursuits.[159] Often the artists most disdainful of the public produce art that is, to put it mildly, a great deal of beauty and hope.

How does Christianity affect an artist's work? This has been and will continue to be a worthy topic for entire books. But in short, the gospel worldview equips the artist, as it does the journalist, for a unique combination of optimism and realism about life. The gospel is more globally pessimistic about human nature than virtually any other view of things. There is no one class or group of people responsible for the world's situation; we all are responsible. Each of us is capable of the worst kind of evil, and there is nothing we can do to change ourselves, or even see ourselves in our true light, without God's help. And yet, on the basis of God's salvation in Christ, the gospel allows us to be at the same time deeply optimistic, envisioning not simply heaven but a perfectly renewed material creation. So artists shaped by the gospel cannot be characterized either by sentimentality or bitter hopelessness.

For example, the movie *Lost in Translation* assumes that life is ultimately meaningless but afford some small comfort in friendship; the movie *Babe* inspires us that even a pig can be a sheepdog if he defies tradition and tries hard enough. I believe that Christians can appreciate either kind of story, if it is well told, because from a gospel perspective, both naive and cynical stories are partly true. Life in this fallen world *is* to a great degree meaningless, our aspirations are constantly being frustrated, and sometimes the respectable people are oppressive and bigoted. And yet there is a Good that will triumph over Evil in the end. From a Christian perspective the problem with both kinds of stories is that they tend to blame problems on things besides sin and identify salvation in things besides God—and therefore are ultimately too simplistic. The richness of the gospel world-story includes the insights of both darker and more sanguine worldviews, and it weaves them into a larger tapestry so that neither overwhelms the whole picture. Christian artists have access to a broader and more balanced vision of the world, which is why, over the centuries, that vision has produced such great works of art.

The Gospel and Medicine

To let the gospel of Jesus shape how we work means to heed the influence of both the psychological idols within our hearts as well as the sociological idols in our culture and profession.[160] For an example of this I will turn to the field of medicine. Some years ago I did an informal survey of several Christians in the medical profession. I asked them, "What are the factors inherent in the practice of medicine today that make it difficult to work as a Christian in this field? What are the main temptations and tests?" I was surprised, instructed, and helped by the answers I received.

One of the main problems mentioned was a deeply personal one—the great temptation to lose sight of your identity in your profession. The British preacher Martyn Lloyd-Jones was previously a successful physician in London. In one of his lectures to medical students and doctors, he said candidly, "there are many whom I have had the privilege of meeting whose tombstones might well bear the grim epitaph . . . 'born a man, died a doctor'! The greatest danger which confronts the [medical professional] is that he may become lost in his profession . . . this is the special temptation of the doctor. . . ."[161] Another British doctor added:

> . . . the temptation [is] for medicine to take over your life and rule your life as an enslaving power. It's a subtle one because . . . there is a kind of moral ego massage because you are giving so much—hours, responsibility, stress—to do so much good in other people's lives. There's a lot of self-justifying power in that kind of idolatry. It's much easier to feel morally superior as a doctor than as a stockbroker. . . . There is also, in some people, the need to be needed and the power buzz you get from having influence. . . .[162]

Those in the helping professions (and that includes pastoral ministry as well as medicine) are tempted to feel superior because our work is so noble and so draining. And although medical professionals pour themselves out in long, stressful hours and literally save lives, they meet plenty of ungrateful, unreasonable, and stubborn people who repay their hard work with venom and lawsuits. This can lead to a correlative spiritual peril. One doctor wrote:

> It is easy to become extremely cynical about people and emotionally hardened to life. You see so much of the messy stuff of life and death that you feel your essential defense mechanism is to become emotionally detached and keep a distance in order to maintain your sanity.

Several doctors told me that only the gospel enabled them to see the traits of pride, cynicism, and detachment that were creeping into their characters. One said, "In the early days of a medical career you work such enormous hours that your prayer life just dries up. That is deadly. Only if Jesus stays real to the heart can you be consistently joyful enough in him to avoid making medicine your whole self-worth, and then becoming hardened when you meet so much ingratitude."

My survey also revealed pressures on doctors that came from the culture. One woman I corresponded with pointed me to an article in *The New England Journal of Medicine* titled "God at the Bedside."[163] The author was a doctor who often found that patients' spiritual beliefs and practices were very much a factor in their health issues, but "in the modern era, religion and science are understood as sharply divided, the two occupying very different domains." He wrote that he often found that patients' guilt and fears were factors in their illness and also that their faith in

God was part of how they healed, but he felt completely unpre-
pared by his training to address any of these realities. "Doctors,"
he wrote, "understandably are leery of moving outside the strictly
clinical and venturing into the spiritual realm."

Dr. Martyn Lloyd-Jones makes the same point in one of his
lectures to medical professionals. Lloyd-Jones was on staff at Saint
Bart's in London under the famous chief of staff Lord Horder in
the late 1920s. At one point the junior physician was asked by Lord
Horder to rearrange and reclassify his case history records. He created a new filing system, arranging the cases not by name but by
diagnosis and treatment. As Lloyd-Jones did this task he was aston-
ished that Horder's diagnostic notes in well over half the cases included comments such as "works far too hard," "drinks too much,"
"unhappy in home and marriage." At one point he spent the weekend with Lord Horder and took the opportunity to ask him about
what he had seen in the case files. Horder responded that he reckoned only about a third of the problems that are brought to a
physician are strictly medical—the rest are due to or aggravated by
anxiety and stress, poor life choices, and unrealistic goals and beliefs
about themselves. Severe cases, of course, could be sent to the psy-
chiatrist, but most of the time that wasn't appropriate. So, Horder
concluded, a doctor should basically mind his or her own business.
Lloyd-Jones said that after he heard that response:

> . . . we argued for the whole of the weekend! My con-
> tention was that we should be treating [the whole of
> the person's life]. "Ah," said Horder, "that is where
> you are wrong! If these people like to pay us our fees
> for more or less doing nothing, then let them do so.
> We can then concentrate on the 35 percent or so of

real medicine." But my contention was that to treat these other people [taking into account their whole life] *was* "real medicine" also. All of them were really sick. They certainly were not well! They have gone to the doctor—perhaps more than one—in quest of help.[164]

Lloyd-Jones was not proposing that physicians were by themselves competent to do this, but rather that together with other counselors and helping professionals they needed to address the whole person. People have a spiritual nature, a moral nature, and a social nature, and if any of these are violated by unwise or wrong beliefs, behaviors, and choices, there can be interlocking physical and emotional breakdown. And even patients whose original illness was caused by strictly physical factors eventually need much more than mere medicine to recuperate and heal.

That conversation took place in 1927, but two trends have only exacerbated the situation that Horder and Lloyd-Jones were addressing. First, there has been an enormous increase in specialization, so that no single helping professional ever seems to have the luxury of looking at the whole person. Just as important is the growth in influence of a view that has been called "evolutionary social constructivism," which believes that "all aspects of every level of reality [have] a single evolutionary explanation."[165] In effect, the very concept of the whole person is vanishing. Our consciousness and emotion, our choices and desires, our goals and joys are increasingly seen to be the results of our genetic hardwiring. The old idea of a person consisting of body, mind, and spirit is gone—now there is only a body that has mental, emotional, and spiritual neurology. In addition to this reductionistic understanding of human nature, the increasing economic and legal pressures on doctors and hospitals are likely to push medical professionals more cautiously to "mind their own business" when it comes to treating the whole person.

Because they understand the effects of both creation and fall on the human person, Christians in the medical profession can resist the narrowing implications of this view. The Christian view of human nature is rich and multifaceted. God created and will resurrect our bodies—and so they are important! If God himself is to redeem our bodies (Romans 8:23) then he is the Great Physician, and the medical vocation could not be loftier. But God does not care only about bodies; he created and redeems our souls as well. So Christian physicians will always bear the totality of the human person in mind. Their faith gives them the resources to muster the humility and the ingenuity necessary to see patients as more than just bodies.

The Christian Worldview Shapes All Work

So when we say that Christians work from a gospel worldview, it does not mean that they are constantly speaking about Christian teaching in their work. Some people think of the gospel as something we are principally to "look at" in our work. This would mean that Christian musicians should play Christian music, Christian writers should write stories about conversion, and Christian businessmen and -women should work for companies that make Christian-themed products and services for Christian customers. Yes, some Christians in those fields would sometimes do well to do those things, but it is a mistake to think that the Christian worldview is operating only when we are doing such overtly Christian activities. Instead, think of the gospel as a set of glasses through which you "look" at everything else in the world. Christian artists, when they do this faithfully, will not be completely beholden either to profit or to naked self-expression; and they will tell the widest variety of stories. Christians in business will see profit as only one of several bottom lines; and they will work passionately for any kind of enterprise that serves the common good. The Christian writer can constantly be showing the destructiveness of making something besides God into the central thing, even without mentioning God directly.

And while the Bible is not a comprehensive handbook for running a business, doing plumbing, or serving patients, it does speak to an enormous range of cultural, political, economic, and ethical issues that are very much part of how we all live. Also, the Christian worldview has made foundational contributions to our own culture that may not be readily apparent. The deep background for our work, especially in the West—the rise of modern technology, the democratic ethos that makes modern capitalism thrive, the idea of inherent human freedom as the basis for economic freedom and the development of markets—is due largely to the cultural changes that Christianity has brought. Historian John Sommerville argues that Western society's most pervasive ideas, such as the idea that forgiveness and service are more important than saving face and revenge, have deeply biblical roots.[166] Many have argued, and I would agree, that the very rise of modern science could have occurred only in a society in which the biblical view of a sole, all-powerful, and personal Creator was prevalent.[167] So we all owe more than we may realize to the unique contours and power of the Christian worldview.

Are you thinking about your work through the lenses of a Christian worldview? Are you asking questions such as:

- What's the story line of the culture in which I live and the field where I work? Who are the protagonists and antagonists?
- What are the underlying assumptions about meaning, morality, origin, and destiny?
- What are the idols? The hopes? The fears?
- How does my particular profession retell this story line, and what part does the profession itself play in the story?
- What parts of the dominant worldviews are basically in line with the gospel, so that I can agree with and align with them?
- What parts of the dominant worldviews are irresolvable without Christ? Where, in other words, must I challenge my culture? How can Christ complete the story in a different way?
- How do these stories affect both the form and the content of my work personally? How can I work not just with excellence but also with Christian distinctiveness in my work?
- What opportunities are there in my profession for (a) serving individual people, (b) serving society at large, (c) serving my field of work, (d) modeling competence and excellence, and (e) witnessing to Christ?

Of all the ways that the Christian faith affects work, the realm of worldview is the most searching and yet also the hardest to put into practice. All Christians live in cultures and work in vocational fields that operate by powerful master narratives that are sharply different from the gospel's account of things. But these narratives work at such a deep level that their effects on us are hard to discern. An American who first moves to a foreign country is shocked to discover how many of her intuitions and practices that she considered common sense and universal are actually particularly American ones—and are ridiculous to many other people. By living in another culture she gets a new vantage point from which she can be critical of herself, and as a result she will slowly change, dropping some attitudes and adopting others.

Becoming a Christian is a lot like moving to a new country; only it is more profound, because it gives us a new perspective on every culture, every worldview, and every field of work. In the long run, the gospel helps us see everything in a new light, but it takes time to grasp and incorporate this new information into how we live and pursue our vocations. And we can be sure that this ultimate learning experience will never truly end; we are told the angels themselves never tire of looking into the gospel to see new wonders (1 Peter 1:10–12).

TEN

A New Conception of Work

Whatever you do, do well.

Ecclesiastes 9:10 (NLT)

Everyone Participates in God's Work

The Jewish community has contributed hugely to the flourishing of New York City. They have led in the advancement of hospitals and medicine, arts and cultural centers, and strong communities that sustain the elderly and nurture the young. Their Scriptural heritage and beliefs give them a strong commitment to "act justly and to love mercy and to walk humbly with your God" (Micah 6:8). They are not Christ followers, but God no doubt continues to work through them. Another group often noted for their commitment to moving to neighborhoods that have fallen into disrepair and rehabilitating them is the gay community. They have worked hard to improve many of the worst parts of our cities over the last several decades. And, of course, we all know someone in our field who is not a Christian who seems to hold the best values and produce the most elegant product, beautiful dance piece, or trusted and well-organized work team. If the Christian worldview is so unique, how do we account for this?

In the last chapter we showed that the gospel provides a worldview, or story, that provides Christian believers with real guidance for their labor, giving them a deep and layered vision of human flourishing that often enables them to work in ways distinct from those around them. But this is not the entire biblical picture. If it were, we might think that non-Christians cannot do good work or good deeds, or that everything a Christian does at their job must be completely and obviously different from everything that a nonbeliever does. That is not the case.

God is Creator of the world, and our work mirrors his creative work when we create culture that conforms to his will and vision for human beings—when it matches up with the biblical story line. Yet theologians speak not only of God's creation but also of his providence. God does not simply create; he also loves, cares for, and nurtures his creation. He feeds and protects all he has made. But how does his providential care reach us? As we have seen in earlier chapters, especially in the teaching of Martin Luther, God's loving care comes to us largely through the labor of others. Work is a major instrument of God's providence; it is how he sustains the human world.

As an extension of God's creative work, the Christian's labor has its orientation toward God himself, and we must ask how it can be done distinctively and for his glory. As an extension of God's providential work, our labor has its orientation toward our neighbor, and we must ask how it can be done excellently and for his or her good. This latter motivation is available to everyone. So a farmer or chef meets her neighbor's need for food; a mechanic meets his neighbor's need for technical help on a car. This aspect of work-as-provision is the reason that much work that Christians do is not done, at least not in its visible form, any differently from the way non-Christians do it. It is not so easy, for example, to identify the uniquely Christian way to fill a cavity. And because *all* human beings are made in the image of God (Genesis 1:26–28) and *all* are given their talents and skills for work in the world by God (1 Corinthians 7:17), we should not be surprised that many people without belief in Jesus can do great work—even better work—than Christians.

In fact, an unbalanced emphasis on worldview has certain dangers. For example, it can lead us to privilege white-collar work over blue-collar work. Writers and managers have the opportunity to think out the influence of Christian beliefs in their work. But how relevant is this to the assembly-line worker or the craftsman or technician, whose worldview may not make an obvious difference to their daily tasks? Of course, all Christians work with radically different inner motives than those who don't believe, and this can certainly make a difference in the quality, spirit, and honesty with which a believer labors. But that does not mean a Christian will build an airplane engine differently from a non-Christian. And so to think of work only in worldview terms, and not in terms of God's providence and love, can subtly imply that the Bible's view of work is less relevant to those of the working classes.

The more serious danger associated with an under-emphasis on work as the vehicle of God's providence is that it leads Christians to undervalue the good work done by nonbelievers.[168] The fullness and balance of the biblical teaching prevents us from valuing only Christian work or only professional work. Instead Christians should place a high value on *all* human work (especially excellent work), done by all people, as a channel of God's love for his world. They will be able to appreciate and rejoice in their own work, whether it is prestigious or not, as well as in the skillful work of all other people, whether they believe or not.

So this biblical conception of work—as a vehicle for God's loving provision for the world—is essential. It counteracts the elitism and sectarianism that can creep into our approach to work when we grasp the distinctiveness of the Christian worldview.

The Balance of Common Grace

When we learn to value all people's work and all kinds of work, we are moving into a realm of Christian theology called "common grace," and at this point it would be good to deepen our understanding of this idea. What can Christians assume they have in common with people who apparently have not experienced saving grace, who are not followers of Jesus? Does God work in the broader reaches of cultural interaction to bestow certain blessings on all people—blessings that provide the basis for Christians to cooperate with, and learn from, non-Christians?[169]

The Bible's answer is "yes." Psalm 19 differentiates between a kind of "wordless speech," which tells all people something about God's presence and glory, and the revelation that comes to believers through the Bible and the convicting work of the Holy Spirit. Romans 1 and 2 confirm that all of us share a primordial knowledge of God: In Romans 2, verses 14–15, Paul says that God's law is written on the heart of every human being. People have innate consciences that are preloaded with senses of honesty, justice, love, the Golden Rule, and so on.[170] People know at some deep level that there is a God, that we are his creatures, that we should serve him, and that he makes demands on us for relationships with him and other people. God further reveals himself to all people through the magnificence of nature—but also through human culture, which is essentially the forming and filling of nature as God created it. Consider Isaiah 28, verses 24–29: "When a farmer plows for planting . . . when he has leveled the surface . . . does he not plant wheat in its place, barley in its plot, and spelt in its field? His God instructs him and teaches him the right way. . . . Grain must be ground to make bread . . . all this also comes from the Lord Almighty, wonderful in counsel and magnificent in wisdom."

This is remarkable. Isaiah tells us that anyone who becomes a skillful farmer, or who brings advancements in agriculture, is being taught by God. One commentator writes of this text, "What appears as a discovery (the proper season and conditions for sowing, farm management, rotation of crops, etc.) is actually the Creator opening his book of creation and revealing his truth."[171]

Remember that farming is an analogue to all culture making. So every advancement in learning, every work of art, every innovation in health care or technology or management or governance, is simply God "opening his book of creation and revealing his truth" to us. Of course, the vast majority of farmers in the history of the world did not know that God was doing this, but Isaiah says that was what was happening. This is what theologians call "general revelation," an aspect of common grace in which God reveals himself to all people. See how other texts from the Bible sound a similar note:

- James 1, verse 17 says that "every good and perfect gift is from above . . . from the Father of the heavenly lights." This means that every act of goodness, wisdom, justice, and beauty—no matter who does it—is being enabled by God. It is a gift, and therefore a form of grace.

- In Exodus 31, verses 1–4, we read how Bezalel was "filled . . . with the Spirit of God, with skill, ability, and knowledge in all kinds of crafts—to make artistic designs." Here we see artistic skill coming from God. Salieri was right—Mozart's music *was* the voice of God, regardless of the moral and spiritual condition of Mozart's heart.
- In Isaiah 45, verse 1, we read of Cyrus, a pagan king whom God anoints with his Spirit and chooses for world leadership. In Genesis 20, verses 6–7 we read how God prevents another pagan king from falling into sin. These are indications of how God's Spirit functions both as a nonsaving *ennobling* force in the world and as a nonsaving *restraining* force in the world. This is not the Spirit working as a converting or a sanctifying agent. Rather he acts to give wisdom, courage, and insight and to restrain the effects of sin—even to those who would deny God's existence.

So through his common grace God blesses all people, so that Christians can benefit from, and cooperate with, non-Christians. However, there are limitations to common grace, which require us to respond to these blessings with balance. In Romans 1, verse 18 Paul says that we "hold the truth in unrighteousness" (KJV). This statement has two edges to it, and John Calvin expresses both well. First he writes about secular authors (he was thinking mainly of the ancient pagan Greek and Roman thinkers):

Let that admirable light of truth shining in them teach
us that the mind of man, though fallen and perverted

from its wholeness, is nevertheless clothed and ornamented with God's excellent gifts. If we regard the Spirit of God as the sole fountain of truth, we shall neither reject the truth itself, nor despise it where it shall appear unless we wish to dishonor the Spirit of God. . . . Those men whom Scripture (1 Corinthians 2:14) calls "natural men" were, indeed, sharp and penetrating in their investigation of inferior things. Let us, accordingly, learn by their example how many gifts the Lord left to human nature even after it was despoiled of its true good.[172]

Here Calvin is appreciating the way God blesses all those who are made in his image. Yet just prior to this, Calvin also writes that while "in man's perverted and degenerate nature some sparks still gleam, [the light is nonetheless] choked with dense ignorance, so that it cannot come forth effectively. [His] mind, because of its dullness . . . betrays how incapable it is of seeking and finding truth."[173]

How could someone write these two seemingly contradictory things within just a few pages of each other? Are nonbelievers capable of discerning the truth or not? Yes and no. Calvin is reading Romans 1 carefully!

First, we must acknowledge that there is no neutrality in the world. Everyone who does not acknowledge Christ as Lord is operating out of a false view of ultimate reality, while to confess Christ as Lord is to be in line with ultimate reality. Everyone is operating from a worldview that either denies Christ or him. No one is objective or neutral; no one can avoid the question.

At the same time, the doctrine of common grace means that

despite all false worldviews, everyone grasps and to some degree acknowledges aspects of the biblical worldview: truths about God, creation, human nature, and our need for rescue. Deep in our hearts' operating systems, God has imprinted his story. This universal knowledge of God and of good—this aspect of natural revelation—has been called "first-order beliefs." All people hold these beliefs at some level, even if their conscious, intellectual, culturally conditioned "second-order beliefs" deny them utterly. Paul says we "hold the truth in unrighteousness"—which means that we all have the truth in some way. How else could we hold it?

This odd tension means that the best of what non-Christians say and do will be based on truths that they "know" at one level and yet do not know at another. For example, Leonard Bernstein's second-order beliefs were secular and naturalistic. But on a TV broadcast he famously said, "Listening to Beethoven's Fifth, you get the feeling there's something right with the world, something that checks throughout, something that follows its own laws consistently, something we can trust, that will never let us down."[174] He was saying that music gave him not simply emotion, but *meaning*. Despite the fact that his formal beliefs were that life was a cosmic accident, and therefore there could be no meaning to anything, music made him feel that there *was* meaning to it all, that it *did* matter how he lived! His first-order beliefs were bubbling up despite his second-order beliefs, as they do for everyone.

The Freedom of Common Grace

Without an understanding of common grace, the world can be a pretty confusing place for a Christian. It would be natural for many Christians to identify with Antonio Salieri: He is bewildered and bitter that as a morally good person, his talent is modest, while Mozart (a morally despicable person, at least in Peter Shaffer's play *Amadeus*) has been favored by God through the gift of his soaring talent. Beyond his blindness to his own sin, Salieri's problem was a failure to understand the reality of common grace. God gives out gifts of wisdom, talent, beauty, and skill according to his grace—that is, in a completely unmerited way. He casts them across the human race like seed, in order to enrich, brighten, and preserve the world. By rights, sin should be making life on earth here much more unbearable than it is—and in fact, all of creation and culture should have fallen apart by now. The reason it is not worse is because of the gift of common grace.

Without an understanding of common grace, Christians will believe they can live self-sufficiently within their own cultural enclave. Some might feel that we should go only to Christian doctors, work only with Christian lawyers, listen only to Christian counselors, or enjoy only Christian artists. Of course, all nonbelievers have seriously impaired spiritual vision. Yet so many of the gifts God has put in the world are given to nonbelievers. Mozart was a gift to us—whether he was a believer or not. So Christians are free to study the world of human culture in order to know more of God; for as creatures made in His image we can appreciate truth and wisdom wherever we find it.

Without an understanding of common grace, Christians will have trouble understanding why non-Christians so often exceed Christians morally and in wisdom. Properly understood, the doctrine of sin means that believers are never as good as our true worldview should make us. Similarly, the doctrine of grace means that unbelievers are never as messed up as their false worldview should make them. For in the Christian story, the antagonist is not non-Christians but the reality of sin, which (as the gospel tells us) lies within us as well as within them.

And so we are likely to be on firm footing if we make common ground with non-Christians to do work that serves the world. Christians' work with others should be marked by both humble cooperation and respectful provocation. An understanding of common grace, as well as an experience of God's pardoning grace in Christ, should lead us to freely and humbly work with others who may not share our faith but can be used greatly by God to accomplish enormous good. At the same time, an understanding of the gospel worldview means we should at times respectfully pursue a different path or winsomely point out how our own Christian faith gives us powerful resources and guidance for what we are doing.[175]

The Dialogue of Popular Culture

In general, Christians' reaction to popular culture in the last eighty years has been some form of disengagement.[176] Music, movies, and television have been sweepingly evaluated as dangerous, polluting, or degrading. The withdrawal has taken different forms. One form is complete renunciation. Another form is the creation of an alternate Christian subculture littered with sanitized, overtly evangelistic forms of music, movies, TV shows, literature, vacation destinations, and so on. A third form of disengagement is uncritical consumption of popular culture without worldview discernment.[177] Why this disengagement with our culture?

One reason is a "thin" or legalistic view of sin, where sin is seen as a series of discrete acts of noncompliance with God's regulations. You pursue Christian growth largely by seeking environments where you are less likely to do these sinful actions or to encounter others who have done them. Sin can essentially be removed from your life through separation and discipline. This view of sin comports with a lack of understanding of the thoroughness and richness of Christ's gracious work for us. For without an understanding of grace we will believe we must (and can) earn our salvation. But to accomplish that we will need a view of sin that is easier to conquer through conscious effort.

If we have a thin view of sin, we will feel safe if we remove from our view anything that could tempt us to commit actions of overt sexual immorality, profanity, dishonesty, or violence. By withdrawing such cultural "texts" from our presence, we may feel less sinful; but we may be fooling ourselves. The complex, organic nature of our sin will still be at work making idols out of good things in our lives—such as our moral goodness, financial security, family, doctrinal purity, or pride in our culture. Of course, there is a great deal that is pernicious in popular culture, with its oft-noted glorification of sex and violence. The Bible tells us to flee sexual temptation (1 Corinthians 6:18–20); and a wise person will set wise boundaries.[178] But too much emphasis on wholesale withdrawal from culture increases the likelihood of slipping into other more "respectable" idolatries. A theologically "thick" view of sin, by contrast, sees it as a compulsive drive of the heart to produce idols. This view should lead neither to withdrawal nor to uncritical consumption, but rather to humble, critical engagement with culture.[178]

Another cause of disengagement is a thin, or intellectualistic, view of common grace. As we noted earlier, all people possess— and suppress—some knowledge of God and his character. But many conceive of this knowledge mainly (or strictly) as cognitive information that can be retrieved and transmitted as we provide evidence of the existence of God, the truth of Christianity, and so on. In other words, we tend to think of this innate knowledge of God in intellectual terms.

But the language of Romans 1, verses 18–25 gives us a much more comprehensive and dynamic picture of how general revelation or common grace works in real life. The truth is being suppressed (verse 18), but it continues to bear down on us. Verse 20 says, "Since the creation of the world God's invisible qualities . . . have been clearly seen, being understood from what has been made, so men are without excuse." But the verbs *nosumena* ("are being understood") and *kathopatai* ("are being seen") are in the form of present passive participles. That is, the reality of God's nature and our obligations to him are continuously presented to us. These realities are not static, propositional information, but rather a continually fresh, insistent pressure on the consciousness of every individual. If this is true, then every artifact of human culture is a positive response to God's general revelation and *simultaneously* a rebellious assertion against his sovereign rule over us (Romans 1:21).

So we can see all cultural production (and remember, everything we do at work is some form of cultural production) as a dialogue between our innate, affirming response to God's common grace and the idolatrous, rebellious nature of our hearts. Therefore, human culture is an extremely complex mixture of brilliant truth, marred half-truths, and overt resistance to the truth. "Loss of faith in a given religion does not by any means imply the eradication of the religious instinct. It merely means that the instinct, temporarily repressed, will seek an object elsewhere."[179]

Here is an interesting example of this dialogue:

One of the movies we have shown students is the Vietnamese/American co-production *Three Seasons,* a collection of four intertwining vignettes. One story has to do with a cyclo (sort of a cross between a bicycle and a rickshaw) driver named Hai and his infatuation with an ambitious prostitute, a young woman who is sure she can sleep her way out of poverty into the cool, clean world of the luxury hotels near where she works. After winning some money in a cyclo race, he pays $50 to spend the night with her. He rents a room in the luxury hotel and the scene leads you to expect a typical, erotic love scene. Against the viewer expectations, though, he does not have sex with her. Instead he simply requests to watch her fall asleep, to watch her rest in the world she dreams of joining. Slowly, comfortably, she falls asleep. And he is gone in the morning, having demanded nothing from her except the chance to fulfill her desire to belong. Something snaps in the prostitute, and she finds she cannot return to her old job. [There is some similarity here to how the grace of the bishop transforms Valjean into an honest man in *Les Misérables.*] It is a powerful scene, a completely unexpected glimpse of fragile beauty and selfless, life-changing love. To my knowledge, director/screenwriter Tony Bui is not a Christian, and perhaps has never even heard the gospel. . . . But moments of beauty and truth [and incredibly poignant images of Christ's saving work] are evidence of the work of God who preserves the noble, creative image of himself in us despite the distorting effects of sin.[180]

Dualism vs. Integration

Christians' disengagement from popular culture usually carries over into dualism at work. "Dualism" is a term used to describe a separating wall between the sacred and the secular. It is a direct result of a thin view of sin, common grace, and God's providential purposes.

Dualism leads some to think that if their work is to please Christ, it must be done overtly in his name. They feel they have to write and perform art that explicitly mentions Jesus, or teach religious subjects in a Christian school; or that they must work in an organization in which all people are professing Christians. Or they must let everyone know that they lead Bible studies in the office in the morning before work hours. (Remember how Luther railed against the separation of all work into the "spiritual estate" and the "temporal estate.") This kind of dualism comes both from a failure to see the panoramic scope of common grace and the subtle depths of human sin. People with this view cannot see that work done by non-Christians always contains some degree of God's common grace as well as the distortions of sin. And they cannot see that work done by Christians, even if it overtly names the name of Jesus, is also significantly distorted by sin.

The opposite dualistic approach, however, is even more prevalent—and based on our experience, even more difficult to dismantle. In this approach, Christians think of themselves as Christians only within church activity. Their Christian life is what they do on Sundays and weeknights, when they engage in spiritual activities. The rest of the week they have no ability to think circumspectly about the underlying values they are consuming and living out. In their life and work "out in the world," they uncritically accept and reenact all of their culture's underlying values and idolatries of self, surface appearances, technique, personal freedom, materialism, and other features of expressive individualism. While the first form of dualism fails to grasp the importance of what we have in *common* with the world, this form fails to grasp the importance of what is *distinctive* about the Christian worldview—namely, that the gospel reframes all things, not just religious things.

The integration of faith and work is the opposite of dualism. We should be willing to be very engaged with the cultural and vocational worlds of non-Christians. Our thick view of sin will remind us that even explicitly Christian work and culture will always have some idolatrous discourse within it. Our thick view of common grace will remind us that even explicitly non-Christian work and culture will always have some witness to God's truth in it. Because Christians are never as good as their right beliefs should make them and non-Christians are never as bad as their wrong beliefs should make them, we will adopt a stance of critical enjoyment of human culture and its expressions in every field of work. We will learn to recognize the half-truths and resist the idols; and we will learn to recognize and celebrate the glimpses of justice, wisdom, truth, and beauty we find around us in all aspects of life. Ultimately, a grasp of the gospel and of biblical teaching on cultural engagement should lead Christians to be the most appreciative of the hands of God behind the work of our colleagues and neighbors.

ELEVEN

A New Compass for Work

On the day of your fasting, you do as you please and ex-
ploit all your workers. . . . Is not this the kind of fasting I
have chosen: to loose the chains of injustice and untie the
cords of the yoke, to set the oppressed free and break every
yoke? Is it not to share your food with the hungry and to
provide the poor wanderer with shelter—when you see the
naked, to clothe him?

Isaiah 58:3, 6–7

The Limitations of Ethics

Not long after the financial meltdown in 2008 and 2009, a writer
in *The New York Times* Sunday Opinion section wrote about a
friend of hers who had worked at an investment bank before she
was laid off. She was known to be hardworking, fair, and honest,
and she had been generous with her money toward friends and
charitable nonprofits. However, her specialty had been securitiz-
ing subprime mortgages, student loans, and credit card debt.
"That all this debt she was putting together like a puzzle and
selling to investors would play such a sinister role in the downfall

of the economy didn't occur to her—although it probably should have."[181] Why didn't it occur to her? So many on Wall Street are asking themselves and one another that question. The reason is that our modern and postmodern idols work against our inclination to ask such questions. They tell us that if the practice is legal and if everyone is doing it, the only fundamental question is: Can money be made?

Some scoff at the idea that the financial services industry and business at large need more external constraints to be ethical. In one article responding to widespread calls for higher ethics among business leaders, *The Economist* cited Milton Friedman's famous dictum that business managers have one and only one goal: to maximize shareholder value.[182] The writer argued that the market itself rewards integrity and punishes dishonesty. No one has to stand over managers and business owners; if they are dishonest it will catch up to them and ruin the bottom line. Pay attention to the bottom line, and the rest will take care of itself.

Indeed, many business ethics courses and books subtly argue in the same way. Yes, they say, business owners and employees should be honest and fair. Yes, we should treat employees with generosity, and we should give back to the community. But why? What is the basis for such an appeal? The most common answer is: It's good for business. It enhances your reputation, and in the long term it creates a more favorable business environment. In other words, most people argue—or at the very least, live out—ethics on the basis of cost-benefit analysis. Integrity is profitable; dishonesty isn't. And most of the time, at least in the long run, this is true.

But is that enough? Won't there be at least some situations in which the short-term gains for an ethically questionable act will be so great, and the danger to you or your friends so small, that on the basis of cost-benefit analysis the potential gains vastly outweigh the risk? Of course. And there will even be situations in any field in which doing the purely ethical thing could be financially ruinous, and, therefore, according to strict cost-benefit analysis, the risk of getting caught in an ethical violation, or fracturing a relationship, is clearly worth taking. So at least part of the time, it is bad business to be honest.

Let's apply this to a more personal and seemingly small situation to which many people can relate. At twenty-seven years old, Howard was given an opportunity to move from one large company to another for a modest increase in responsibility, but greater future opportunity. At the point of salary negotiations, Howard was asked to share his current salary with his prospective employer. Howard pumped up the figure by a mere 4 percent, a few thousand dollars. Of course his thinking was that the higher they thought his salary was currently, the more they'd offer him. He justified the lie because the prospective company offered two weeks less vacation a year than his current one. He just added the value of that benefit onto his salary figure. On the very slim chance that he'd get caught, he had a plausible excuse. The benefit outweighed the cost and risk. And by the way, he was pretty sure everyone did this sort of thing. So was there anything wrong with it?

Our individual professional ethics have a cumulative effect, for good or ill, on the broader common good. In a short but compelling booklet, former vice president of the European Parliament Sir Fred Catherwood contends that corruption is one of the greatest challenges to economic development and political stability in the world.[183] As a young man in an international construction business, he discovered that bribery was routine in the parts of the world in which there was little political stability and terrible extremes of wealth and poverty, but where it was less prevalent both the economy and civil society were stronger. In response to this pattern, representatives of many international companies, development institutions, public officials, and other NGOs created an anticorruption movement called Transparency International.[184]

Catherwood tells a story to illustrate that personal honesty has a wider social impact, and also that practicing honesty takes not just an individual but the support of the entire community. He relates the experience of a brilliant young Christian doctor from a country where, by law, hospital care was supposed to be free to all citizens. The reality was that both nurses and doctors were routinely bribed in order to secure care, and therefore only the wealthy got treatment. Many died because they could not pay. This evil was systemic, because the government could not supply the kind of financial support necessary to provide the hospital care it promised, in large part due to corruption and payoffs in other parts of the political structure. The young man refused, for the sake of conscience, to take the bribes, and so he essentially could not participate in the health care program of his society. When he looked to his church for support, he was disappointed. The rapidly growing national church was still young and not yet socially secure. They were afraid to oppose the powerful government interests. In frustration he finally emigrated, leaving behind the country that so greatly needed both his skills and his commitment to justice.[185]

Paul Batchelor of Transparency International warns that most people believe corruption to be a problem only in "backward" parts of the world. That is a gross oversimplification, as he writes in an essay called "Salt and Light: Christians' Role in Combating Corruption."[186] The greater the corruption, the greater the economic weakness. But even in the more prosperous parts of the world corruption saps economies that could be even stronger and robs many people—usually the poor—of the benefits of living in those societies. Batchelor points to our growing awareness that in the financial world there is often "distortion of investment and incentives," such that investors and shareholders can no longer trust the numbers that companies and financial institutions give them, and this lack of trust undermines investment and growth. The week I am writing this, Barclays Bank has been fined more than 450 million dollars for manipulating the prices of financial products to their own benefit (in this case by rigging the Libor, or London Interbank Offered Rate) and to the detriment of small businesses and investors.[187]

Batchelor points out that corruption does not mark only the business world. He lists revelations of corruption, outright bribery, and gross self-interest by elected and government officials. This leads to increasing cynicism on the part of the citizenry, and less participation in the political process, which then enables corruption to thrive all the more. Hugh Heclo, professor of government at Harvard and George Mason, wrote a book called *On Thinking Institutionally* that traces the history of the steady loss of confidence that Americans have experienced toward all of their institutions—government, business, religious—and the consequent dire effects on society.[188] So personal dishonesty in the workplace—when it breeds—can have far wider effects on society.

So what about Howard? How could his small lie possibly have wider effects on society? As Howard tells the story now, he shares that a real breakthrough in his thinking happened when he realized that the desire for just a little more money would so easily cause him to forsake his integrity. Why couldn't he just have been honest and shared that he thought the two weeks' vacation he'd be sacrificing was worth an additional few thousand dollars? Why couldn't he just trust that God, who was providing the interview in the first place, would provide for the salary? And was he basing his interest in the job on the salary or on the work God was giving him to do? He realized that the wider impact on society started with the recognition that, with integrity sacrificed on the altar of money, the next lie would be easier. He realized that others who might observe him could be tempted to do the same. Everyone would trust one another a little less. And he realized that to work for the money instead of the value that the work itself might contribute would damage the culture of the company he was joining.

Christians can take a stand against unethical behavior, even if it means great sacrifice on their part. Fortunately, the story line of the Christian faith gives believers an ethical bedrock—a much firmer foundation for acting with integrity than offered by the pragmatic approach of a cost-benefit analysis. We are to be honest, compassionate, and generous not because these things are rewarding (which they usually are, hence the cost-benefit approach to ethics), but because they are right in and of themselves—because to do so honors the will of God and his design for human life. Sometimes, of course, that will put us in the minority and even at a disadvantage. But indeed, as Bible scholar Bruce Waltke points out, the Bible says that the very definition of righteous people is that they disadvantage themselves to advantage others, while "the wicked . . . are willing to disadvantage the community to advantage themselves."[189]

A Different Set of Virtues

In Chapter 10 we argued that the biblical concept of common grace emphasizes the commonalities between Christians and our work colleagues who do not subscribe to our beliefs. So Christians and non-Christians can share the same education and expertise, can appreciate together advances in the field and admire the most skilled practitioners, whatever their faith. It is important to be as skillful, diligent, savvy, and disciplined as we can possibly be. In Colossians 3, verse 23 we are told "whatever you do, work at it with all your heart, as working for the Lord." Those who take this biblical directive seriously will seek the respect of their colleagues for the quality and integrity of their work. This means having a track record of saying what we mean and doing what we say, following through on commitments every time, whether formal or informal, and being transparent and fair-minded.

Many argue that being a person of integrity and dedication is simply common sense, that it does not require Christian faith. At one level this is true. The well-known appendix to C.S. Lewis's *The Abolition of Man* demonstrates how similar various cultures and religions are in their understanding of the virtuous human life.[190] Nonetheless, Christians are equipped with an ethical compass and power of the gospel that can set us apart—sometimes sharply, sometimes subtly—from those around us. This is because biblical Christian faith gives us significant resources not present in other worldviews, which, if lived out, will differentiate believers in the workplace.

Thomas Aquinas, the greatest Christian theologian of the medieval era, looked at the four cardinal virtues of Plato—justice, courage, temperance, and prudence—and agreed that these were also taught in the Christian Scriptures.[191] Then Aquinas added three theological virtues—faith, hope, and love—to the four cardinal virtues, because these are specifically and uniquely born out of the Christian revelation about the character of God and his grace. While ancient cultures certainly valued compassion within limits, Christian teaching raised the definition of the idea of love to a new level, to include loving one's enemies and forgiving persecutors. This was seen as outrageous by those in shame and honor cultures, where vengefulness was seen as a virtue.

French philosopher Luc Ferry in his history of philosophy argues that Christianity got "the upper hand over Greek thought and dominated Europe" especially because of what it taught "in the realm of ethics." Specifically, Greek thought had always seen ultimate reality as fundamentally impersonal, but "the harmonious and divine structure of the *cosmos* . . . came to be identified for Christians with a single and unique personality, that of Christ."[192] Before Christianity, both Western and Eastern cultures conceived of salvation as entrance into an impersonal and anonymous state. There was no concept that we came from divine love and could return to experience it. But Christianity understood ultimate reality to be rooted in a personal God who created out of love. This caused "the transition from an anonymous and blind doctrine of salvation to one that promises not only that we shall be saved by one person, Christ, but that we shall be saved as individuals in our own right."[193]

Christians understood that we were made by and for eternal love, which was the primary meaning of life. Even the Christian doctrine of God as triune, consisting of three persons who have known and loved one another from all eternity, demonstrates that relationships of love are the building blocks of all reality. And the ultimate purpose of God's work of creation was to create a world of persons with whom he could enjoy a relationship. God created people, not to receive love and honor from them but to share the love, joy, honor, and glory he already had within the Trinity.[194]

Love, then, occupies a supreme place in the Christian imagination. As Jesus says, to be fully human boils down to loving God and loving our neighbor. Everything else—our accomplishments, our causes, our identity, and our feelings—is a distant second. Of course this understanding of the nature of reality will have an extensive impact on how we do our work. For instance, are relationships a means to the end of accruing power, wealth, and comfort? Or is wealth creation a means to serve the end goal of loving others? One way goes against the grain of the universe made by a triune God, and therefore it cannot honor him or lead to human flourishing. The other is the paradigm of Christian work.

Think of the cliché that nobody ever gets to the end of their life and wishes they had spent more time at the office. It makes good sense, of course, up to a point. But here's a more interesting perspective: At the end of your life, will you wish that you had plunged more of your time, passion, and skills into work environments and work products that helped people to give and receive more love? Can you see a way to answer "yes" to this question from your current career trajectory?

A Different View of Humanity

Together with the supremacy of love, Christian faith gives us another resource for ethical behavior—a specific basis for honoring human rights. If every person is made in the image of God he or she has inviolable rights, regardless of that person's race, class, gender, lifestyle, or moral character. Ferry says that among the Greeks and Romans, the worth of a person rested in his inherited gifts and abilities, not simply in being human.[195] This is the reason Aristotle could write that some people are naturally born to be slaves, because they were not as capable of advanced rational thought. He said, "Nature would like to distinguish between the bodies of freemen and slaves, making the one strong for servile labor, the other upright, and although useless for such services, useful for political life in the arts both of war and peace. . . . It is clear, then, that some men are by nature free, and others slaves, and that for these latter slavery is both expedient and right."[196]

By stark contrast, John Calvin, one of the Protestant Reformers, wrote:

> The great part of [men] are most unworthy if they be judged by their own merit. But here Scripture helps in the best way when it teaches that we are not to consider that men merit of themselves but to look upon the image of God in all men, to which we owe all honor and love. . . . You will say, "He has deserved something far different of me." Yet what has the Lord deserved? . . . Remember not to consider men's evil intention but . . . look upon the image of God in them, which . . . with its beauty and dignity allures us to love and embrace them.[197]

By resting its case upon a unique definition of the human person (as image-bearer of God) and an unprecedented idea of love (as the origin, purpose, and destiny of the world), Christianity was to have an incalculable effect upon the history of ideas and the development of culture. If not for the Christian view of the individual, for example, the philosophy of human rights to which we subscribe today would never have emerged. Christianity held that *all* human beings are made in the image of God and therefore have an inviolable right to be treated with honor and love, regardless of whether they culturally, morally, and personally appeal to or offend us. The sweeping nature of this ethical principle is startling, and nothing of its kind was produced in pre-Christian cultures. As Ferry notes and others have argued extensively, this understanding of human rights grew out of the soil of the Christian belief in the image of God.[198]

How should this belief be manifest in the way Christians do their work? Katherine has shared that when she first made the switch from business to working in the church, she was talking to a pastor colleague about some of her "contacts" in town. The pastor turned to her and gently said, "Katherine, you work in ministry now. In ministry we call them 'people.'" The pressures and practices of the marketplace increasingly cause us to rationalize every aspect of life by analyzing efficiencies. People become contacts who can help you; customers are eyeballs and wallets; employees are resources to execute a task. It's so easy to measure the worth of customers, employees, and even congregants in financial terms. From a strictly economic perspective, shareholders, management, employees, suppliers, customers, and community residents have unequal financial value, and it is difficult not to treat them unequally in some respects. But while economically speaking some are more valuable than others, theologically speaking all of us are made in the image of God and are therefore equal in importance.

Consider the case of an unavoidable layoff. Of course, at various times in any community's life some stakeholders need to sacrifice for the long-term good of the whole. Nevertheless it is possible to handle these situations with love. Managers leading in a layoff situation can minimize their own time, discomfort, and effort by issuing terse bulletins and shutting off any ability to question or express concerns. But treating people as human beings with dignity rather than interchangeable resources means being transparent with information, offering extensive two-way communication, and seeking genuinely to persuade rather than merely to control people's responses. Treating people with dignity in the midst of the reality of downsizing and layoffs requires a strong moral compass. But belief in the image of God can bring a new dimension to the conduct of organizational life.

As Ferry and others observe, the concept of human rights, born out of the theological virtue of love, has been appropriated and deployed widely today by many people who do not believe in Christianity or indeed in God at all. Millions of irreligious people can and do believe passionately in human rights. But some have also warned that in a thoroughly secular society, without the belief in a loving, personal God from which the whole concept came, long-term commitment to human rights could wane. Christians must remain absolutely committed to an understanding of human rights based on the image of God.[199]

A Different Source of Guidance

Most people think of faith and spirituality as consisting of doctrinal beliefs, moral behavior, and spiritual experience. So when thinking of God giving us a "moral compass," they imagine a set of ethical rules and regulations, a kind of divine instruction manual from God for life. And it is certainly true that in the Bible Christians receive many practical ethical principles for how to live and many boundary markers showing us what behavior we must completely avoid. If that were all God provided us, it would be helpful, but insufficient. Because there is a whole category missing—*wisdom.*

According to the Bible, wisdom is more than just obeying God's ethical norms; it is knowing the right thing to do in the 80 percent of life's situations in which the moral rules don't provide the clear answer. There is no biblical law that tells you what job to take, whether to go back to school, whom to marry and befriend, when to speak out or hold your peace, whether to make the deal or walk away—yet the wrong decisions can blow up your life.

How can we become wise so that we make good decisions? The Bible teaches that wisdom accumulates from several sources. First, we must not merely believe in God, but know him personally. When God's gracious love becomes not an abstract doctrine but a living reality, it means our heart is less controlled by anxiety and pride, two powerful forces that constantly lead us to unwisely over- or under-react to situations. Second, we must know ourselves. Many bad decisions stem from an inability to know what we are and are not capable of accomplishing. The gospel keeps us from over- or underestimating our own abilities, because it shows us both our sin and God's love for us in Christ. Third, we learn wisdom through experience. The foolish heart—blinded from reality because of its idols—does not learn from experience. In fact, the ups and downs of life can lead us to many false inferences. The proud person blames all failures on others, while the self-hater takes full blame for them even when others are responsible. Without the knowledge of God and self that the gospel brings, experience may teach us precious little; but if we know God and self, then time deepens our understanding of human nature, of the times we live in, of the power and use of words, of how human relationships work. All this leads to wisdom in decision-making.

In the Old Testament, the best place to understand wisdom is the book of Proverbs. Proverbs is a rich resource for handling anger, envy, pride, and discouragement; for resisting the temptations of beauty, money, and power; for wrestling with the problem of self-control; for making decisions; and for keeping relationships in good repair. And what does the New Testament teach? It assumes all the Old Testament teaches about the nature of wisdom, but it gives Christians a new and wonderful resource to do what Proverbs calls us to do. How can we move from merely knowing about God to knowing God? How can we get deep insight into our own heart and the hearts of others? The answer is through the Holy Spirit, given to us by Christ when we embrace him in faith.

The New Testament calls the Holy Spirit the "spirit of wisdom" (Ephesians 1:17) and "power" (1:19). Paul prays for his friends that God would fill them with "all the wisdom and understanding that the Spirit gives" (Colossians 1:9). When he speaks in the famous Ephesians 5 passage about being filled with the

Spirit he calls his readers to "be very careful . . . how you live—not as unwise but as wise" (Ephesians 5:15–16).[200] To be wise is to know how to best use every moment strategically. And this insight comes from the influence of the Holy Spirit, who also strengthens us to live a life worthy of the Lord (Colossians 1:11) and is referred to as a "spirit of power, of love, and of self-discipline" (2 Timothy 1:7).

But how does the Spirit come to give us wisdom? Are we to sit in silence and wait to hear a voice? Not at all. In Acts 15 we see the leaders of the early church embroiled in a controversy over whether Gentile converts were required to keep the Jewish dietary laws and other cultural customs. In effect, they were wrestling with an issue of organizational policy. The text shows us that they debated and discussed matters intensely until they came up with a solution. Then they made a decision and sent it out to the church with the fascinating words, "It seemed good to the Holy Spirit and to us that . . ." (Acts 15:28). In other words, they used their best thinking and reasoning, their knowledge and their experience, and came up with a sound decision that they attributed to the Holy Spirit.

Here then is how the Spirit makes us wise. On the night before he died, Jesus told his disciples that he would send the Holy Spirit and "when he, the Spirit of truth, comes . . . he will glorify me . . ." (John 16:13–14). The Spirit does not make us wise in some magical kind of way, giving us little nudges and insider tips to help us always choose the best stock to invest in. Rather, he makes Jesus Christ a living, bright reality, transforming our character, giving us new inner poise, clarity, humility, boldness, contentment, and courage. All of this leads to increasing wisdom as the years go by, and to better and better professional and personal decisions.

A Different Audience

In Ephesians 6, Paul sets forth a simple but profound principle that both ennobles work (for those in danger of viewing it as drudgery) and demythologizes work (for those in danger of making it their identity). He says all work should be done "as if you were serving the Lord":

> Slaves, obey your earthly masters with respect and fear, and with sincerity of heart, just as you would obey Christ. Obey them not only to win their favor when their eye is on you, but as slaves of Christ, doing the will of God from your heart. Serve wholeheartedly, as if you were serving the Lord, not people, because you know that the Lord will reward each one for whatever good they do, whether they are slave or free. And masters, treat your slaves in the same way. Do not threaten them, since you know that he who is both their Master and yours is in heaven, and there is no favoritism with him (Ephesians 6:5–9).

Paul is speaking to servants and masters, and this raises many questions in the minds of modern readers about the Bible's depiction of the evil of slavery. While much can be said about this subject,[201] it is important to remember that slavery in the Greco-Roman world was not the same as the New World institution that developed in the wake of the African slave trade. Slavery in Paul's time was not race-based and was seldom lifelong. It was more like what we would call indentured servitude. But for our purposes, think of this passage as a rhetorical amplifier and consider this: If *slave owners* are told they must not manage workers in pride and through fear, how much more should this be true of employers today? And if *slaves* are told it is possible to find satisfaction and meaning in their work, how much more should this be true of workers today?

The key to Paul's teaching here is psychological as well as spiritual. He tells both employees and employers to change their audience. Who is watching you work? Whom are you working for? Whose opinion matters most in the end?

For employees. First, workers are told to be wholehearted in their work ("with sincerity of heart," verse 5). They are not to do only the minimum work necessary to avoid penalty; they are not to work hard only when their supervisors can observe them; nor are they to work mindlessly or distractedly. Instead Christians are to be fully engaged at work as whole persons, giving their minds, hearts, and bodies fully to doing the best job possible on the task at hand. Why?

Christian workers can think and work this way because they have a new motive for their work. They work "as if [they] were serving the Lord" (verse 5). So because they have an unimaginable reward in Christ (verse 8), their work does not have to be unduly tied to the amount of reward that they get from their masters. A parallel passage reads, "Whatever you do, work at it with all your heart, as working for the Lord, not for men, since you know that you will receive an inheritance from the Lord as a reward" (Colossians 3:23–24). The Greek word "an" before "inheritance" should really be translated as "the." Paul is talking about the bliss of the world to come.

Christians, you see, have been set free to enjoy working. If we begin to work as if we were serving the Lord, we will be freed from both overwork and underwork. Neither the prospect of money and acclaim, nor the lack of it, will be our controlling consideration. Work will be primarily a way to please God by doing his work in the world, for his name's sake.

Once Christian workers understand this principle, there are several practical implications. First, they are to serve with "respect and fear"—a phrase that means on one hand being courteous and respectful (rather than disdainful) and on the other hand humbly confident (rather than cringing or servile). The term "fear" probably means "the fear of the Lord." In the Bible, this does not mean to cower in terror of God. Passages such as Psalm 130, verse 4 teach that the more you experience God's mercy and forgiveness, the more the true fear of the Lord will increase in you. This true fear of God means to live in such awe and wonder, and in such intense love and respect, that you fear to dishonor him or grieve him. Imagine having in your home someone whom you have admired all your life and whom you never thought you would meet. You revere the person by reputation, so you will not act casually; you will make every effort to fulfill his or her every request and wish. This is how we are to regard God's interest in our work. Work is to be done with all your heart and might, as skillfully as you can, and it should feel not like a burden, but a privilege.

Second, Christians are to work with "sincerity of heart," which is literally *singleness* of heart, a term that connotes both focus and integrity. It means our work must be ethical, not dishonest or duplicitous in any regard. Third, we are to work "not only to win their favor when their eye is on you." This means we do not work hard only when being watched; nor do we do only what is necessary to get by. Finally, the word "wholeheartedly" in verse 7 means Christians are to work with cheerfulness and joy.

For employers. Here Paul tells masters that they are slaves too—slaves of Christ (verse 9). That is an extraordinary and radical word to speak into a rigidly hierarchical culture. He is saying, "Conduct yourself among your servants as if you are a fellow slave"! It is easy to overlook the little phrase "in the same way." In what way? In the way that slaves were to treat their masters—with the greatest respect for their needs! New Testament scholar Peter O'Brien writes:

> In what is a shocking exhortation to slave owners in the first-century Greco-Roman world, the apostle admonishes masters: *treat your slaves in the same way.* According to a proverbial statement known to Seneca, "all slaves are [our] enemies," while many masters were tyrants and abusive. In order to deal with their slaves, owners were known to threaten beatings, sexual harassment, or selling male slaves away from the households with the result that they would be parted forever from their loved ones. Paul's cryptic exhortation is outrageous. It does not mean, however, that masters are to serve their slaves. . . . likely it points to their *attitudes and actions*, which, like those of slaves, are to be *governed* by their relationship to their heavenly Lord. An outcome of this will be that masters will abandon the use of threats against their slaves. This is not to suggest that slaves could not be warned of punishment if they did wrong. Rather, the clause rejects all forms of manipulating, demeaning, or terrifying slaves

by threats. In the immediate context, slaves have already been instructed to show respect, sincerity of
heart, and goodwill; now masters are urged to treat
them in a similar manner.[202]

Paul's reason for this radical attitude is not only that they are
equal as slaves before the Lord, but also that the Lord (to whom
all are equally accountable) is impartial. There is no favoritism
with him. God treats no one differently on the basis of race, class,
or education. As Romans 3 shows us, all are equally judged guilty
and all can equally receive grace through faith. Paul is telling
masters in the strongest way, "Don't think of yourself as a better
person, in better spiritual condition, than your laborers and slaves."

Once Christian employers and leaders grasp these principles,
several practical implications follow. First, "do not threaten
them" means that employers are not to use guilt and coercion to
motivate people. We cannot assume that every servant addressed
in this letter had Christian masters or that the masters had Christian slaves. So these masters could not assume that their servants
were "working as if they were serving God." Nevertheless,
whether the servant is a Christian or not, employers are told here
not to rely primarily on fear as a motivation for work. Second,
"treat your slaves in the same way" means, "Look for ways to
further the interests of the people under your leadership even as
I just charged them to seek to serve you." This means you take
an interest in them as people and invest in their whole lives, not
just their productive work capacity. Third, Paul reminds them
that class distinctions make no difference to God, and therefore
they should not make much difference to us. Masters are not to
be condescending, demeaning, or haughty.

We all work for an audience, whether we are aware of it or not. Some perform to please parents, others to impress peers, others to win over superiors, while many do what they do strictly to live up to their own standards. All of these audiences are inadequate. Working for them alone will lead to overwork or underwork—sometimes a mixture of the two, based on who is watching. But Christians look to an Audience of One, our loving heavenly Father, and that gives us both accountability and joy in our work.

The Orientation of a New Compass

If Christians are animated by different virtues, lifted by a different view of humanity, guided by a different source of wisdom, and perform for a different audience, what will be different about the way they act at work? Let me propose a handful of examples.

Christians should be known to *not be ruthless*. They should have a reputation for being fair, caring, and committed to others. They should be marked by sympathy and by an unusual willingness to forgive and reconcile. There should be a lack of vengefulness, sanctimony, and spite.

Years ago I heard one unforgettable example of a Christian who showed this kind of integrity and compassion. Not long after we began our new church in New York City, I saw a young woman who was obviously visiting and darting out after each service. One week I intercepted her. She told me she was exploring Christianity. She didn't believe in it at that point, but she found a lot of it interesting. I asked her how she had found Redeemer, and she told me this story.

She worked for a company in Manhattan, and not long after

starting there she made a big mistake that she thought would cost her the job, but her boss went in to his superior and took complete responsibility for what she had done. As a result, he lost some of his reputation and ability to maneuver within the organization. She was amazed at what he had done and went in to thank him. She told him that she had often seen supervisors take credit for what she had accomplished, but she had never seen a supervisor take the blame for something she had done wrong. She wanted to know what made him different. He was very modest and deflected her questions, but she was insistent. Finally he told her, "I am a Christian. That means among other things that God accepts me because Jesus Christ took the blame for things that I have done wrong. He did that on the cross. That is why I have the desire and sometimes the ability to take the blame for others." She stared at him for a long moment and asked, "Where do you go to church?" He suggested she go to Redeemer, and so she did. His character had been shaped by his experience of grace in the gospel, and it made his behavior as a manager attractive and strikingly different from that of others. This lack of self-interest and ruthlessness on the part of her supervisor was eventually life-transforming to her.

In addition, Christians should be known to be *generous*, and in the workplace this expresses itself in many ways. As business managers, they can be generous with their time and investment in their employees and customers. As small business owners, they can take less personal profit in order to give customers better value and employees better pay. As citizens they can be discernibly generous with their time and money, giving away more of their income than others in their economic position. They can consider living modestly, below their potential lifestyle level, in order to be financially generous with others.

Christians should be also known to be *calm and poised in the face of difficulty or failure.* This may be the most telling way to judge if a person is drawing on the resources of the gospel in the development of personal character. In Matthew 6, verses 19 and 21 Jesus says, "Do not store up for yourselves treasures on earth, where moths and vermin destroy, and where thieves break in and steal. . . . For where your treasure is, there your heart will be also." What does he mean? Everyone has treasures—the things we cherish, delight in, and adore above all other things. We've also called them idols, and to understand them is to understand much of the hierarchy of your soul and the foundation of your personality. If we get our main meaning from peer approval, or money in the bank, or our reputation for success—then these things are our treasures. But Jesus rightly points out how radically insecure we are if we treasure such things. They can be whisked away or stolen.[203] And then our very lives can fall apart.

This is why for so many people the prospect of career reversal or business failure is such a struggle. When our meaning in life and identity is at stake, we panic, often acting impulsively, sometimes finding ourselves able to lie and betray others in order to save ourselves, or we simply plunge into despair. But Jesus says, rather, "store up for yourselves treasures in heaven" (verse 20). What does that mean? Paul tells us that in Christ all treasures are hid (Colossians 2:3), and Peter says that Jesus was rejected for us, dying to take what we deserved, and therefore "to you who believe, [he] is precious" (1 Peter 2:7). (In fact, Peter uses the noun form, saying literally, "He is preciousness." Jesus is the standard by which things can be called valuable.) This is not simply rhetoric or even abstract theology. The Bible is saying: Only if Jesus is your treasure are you truly rich, for he is the only currency that cannot be devalued. And only if he is your Savior are you truly successful, for status with him is the only status that can't be lost.

Finally, Christians should not be seen as *sectarian*. Many Christians fail to identify themselves as Christians to their colleagues. They simply blend in. Others let their faith be known but speak and act in a way that makes nonbelievers feel subtly (or overtly) marginalized or disdained. But if we have an integrated and non-dualistic understanding of work, we know that many people who are not believers are, through God's providence and common grace, given the gifts to do excellent work. So we will respect and treat those who believe differently as valued equals in the workplace—and at the same time we will be unashamed to be identified with Jesus. If a Christian avoids both of these errors, he or she will be striking an unusual and healthy balance.

I know a man who began a business some years ago based on the idea that in a particular sector of financial services the existing providers of a particular product were using the complexity of the instruments and the ignorance of customers to keep prices high. He believed that a new company, being more transparent with clients, could offer lower prices and better service, not only resulting in healthy profits, but also helping bring reform and integrity to a field that sorely needed them. When he presented his idea to prospective partners and employees, he struck a remarkable balance. He said that the new company was going to be values-driven, and he laid out those values. He stressed that he was committed to these values not merely because they would attract clients and drive revenue, but also because they were the right things to do. He said that these values grew out of his own Christian faith but, he quickly added, regardless of the basis for anyone else's beliefs, if they were committed to the same values, they were equal partners. This is an excellent example of being both open about one's faith and yet nonexclusive or sectarian about it. It's hard to do, and it's rare; but it can be such a potent force for good in the workplace.

Christian Ethics in Your Vocation

Even when Christians are working with integrity inside systems that are not inherently corrupt, it is important for them to ask larger questions about the ordinary ways that work is done in their vocation. In particular, Christians must always be exploring—in communities of faith and practice—how it would be possible for their field of work to be more just and beneficial to more people.

So, for example, Christian economist Michael Schluter sums up the criticisms that Christians and others have leveled at capitalism in its present-day form.[204] Nearly all the problems usually cited stem from the loss of the primacy of human relationships. First, the increasing size and global reach of companies distances investors and decision makers from local communities. So, for example, the directors of the banks of Baltimore traditionally lived in Baltimore and served on the boards of the hospitals, museums, and other cultural institutions there. Now, the senior executives of the banks of Baltimore live in Charlotte, New York City, or London. They are almost completely disconnected from the needs of the communities in which so many employees and customers live.

Second, the risk involved in loaning money is shrinking—sometimes to the point of zero—due to government bailouts and highly complex financial instruments. This means there are practically no repercussions for bad investments or loans. For example, if you were a local banker, and you were asked for a mortgage loan by a would-be homeowner you knew and for a small business loan by a would-be entrepreneur you knew, you would do all you could to assess whether the loan would be fruitful. Will it enable the homeowner to increase her equity? Will the new business succeed and create wealth and jobs in the town? As a banker, your downside for a bad decision would be evident. In today's environment, all parties are faceless to one another, and the old accountability system for punishing bad investments and rewarding good ones is evaporating.

Third, there is the increasing tendency, based on the factors discussed previously, for managers in pursuit of profit to take actions to boost their share price quickly at the expense of the company's long-term health, and also at the expense of its workers, its customers, and the environment. They can cash out and leave everyone else poorer, and the stigma of doing so grows weaker ever year.

Finally, there is the trend of what sociologists call "commodification," which is defined as ascribing monetary value and applying cost-benefit analysis to such things as relationships, family, and civic engagement. The values of the market inexorably intrude on all of life. For example, accidents and tragedies were once dealt with through community support and spiritual disciplines, but now in the age of litigation, "mental distress" must be assigned some kind of objective financial value. So pain gets a number; then in court the number is argued over. How great was the litigant's pain and suffering? How much money will it take to deal with it? A recent book, *The Outsourced Self: Intimate Life in*

Market Times, says that private family life is no longer, as historian and cultural critic Christopher Lasch named it, "a haven in a heartless world." The book description summarizes a point that many have been making for a generation:

> The family has long been a haven in a heartless world, the one place immune to market forces and economic calculations, where the personal, the private, and the emotional hold sway. Yet . . . that is no longer the case: everything that was once part of private life—love, friendship, child rearing—is being transformed into packaged expertise to be sold back to confused, harried Americans. . . . [This volume] follows the incursions of the market into every stage of intimate life. From dating services that train you to be the CEO of your love life to wedding planners who create a couple's "personal narrative"; from nameologists (who help you name your child) to wantologists (who help you name your goals); from commercial surrogate farms in India to hired mourners who will scatter your loved one's ashes in the ocean of your choice . . . the most intuitive and emotional of human acts have become work for hire.[205]

As we have seen, the triune nature of God, and our being made in his image, means that human life is fundamentally relational. But contemporary capitalism increasingly has the power to eliminate the intimacy and accountability of human relationships. So in the marketplace, as in every field, there is an urgent need for those with a powerful compass.

Theological and ethical reflection on our field of work is not easy. It is easier by far to focus on your own job and merely seek to work with personal integrity, skill, and a joyful heart. That is indeed a major part of what it means for a Christian to do faithful work, but that is not all it takes. Christians are to think persistently and deeply about the shape of work in their field and whether (in biblical terms) it accords as well as possible with human well-being and with justice.[206]

And if it doesn't, what should you do? Most people just beginning their career are not in a position to make any kind of broader changes to their field or work environment. But if you have done the work of sustained reflection, then when you begin to accumulate more power and influence—and especially if you are able to begin a new enterprise or business yourself—it may be possible to make significant changes to how work is done in such a way that it influences your profession. You might help lead a financial services or IT company that delivers such an unusual amount of transparency to shareholders and customers that it forces other companies to operate with more integrity. You might form a film production company, start a school, or run an art gallery—combining excellence and values in such a way that it has an impact on many others who are working in the field. These moves would allow you to "serve the work" at a whole new level. None of this will happen, however, unless you begin thinking deeply about your kind of work now. Only then will you be ready to make the changes if and when the opportunity presents itself. Work in the hope that God will open such doors for you in the future.

TWELVE

New Power for Work

Whatever you do, work at it with all your heart.

Colossians 3:23

The Work Under the Work

After finishing her psychiatry residency, a young doctor was working at a New York City hospital. She was friends with a doctor who was a few years ahead of her and who was pregnant with her second child. "Do you know what I love most about being pregnant?" the older doctor said to her friend one day. "I love being pregnant because it's the only time where I feel productive *all* the time. Even when I'm sleeping, I'm *doing* something!" It struck the young M.D. that her friend based her self-regard so completely on productivity that she seemed relieved to finally find a task she could do incessantly. She reflected, "For many of us, being productive and *doing* becomes . . . an attempt at *redemption*. That is, through our work, we try to build our worth, security, and meaning."[207]

Many people are trying to get a sense of self through productivity and success—but that burns them out. For others the mo-

[*226*]

tivation is to bring home a paycheck so they can enjoy "real life"—but that makes work into a pointless grind. These motivations are what we could call the "work beneath the work." And they are what make work so physically and emotionally exhausting in the end.

Though Jesus' twelve apostles left their nets after meeting him (Luke 5:11), we later see them continuing their trade of fishing. We see Paul continuing to work as a tent maker while he worked as an evangelist. These are not men who meet Christ and stop their "secular work" or who dial back their intensity and passion. Instead, what forever changed was the disciples' *relationship* to their work. Jesus gave them the big picture; in fact, he was the big picture. He very deliberately called them to a kind of fishing beyond their fishing: "Don't be afraid; from now on you will fish for people" (Luke 5:11). In other words, he was coming to redeem and heal the world, and he invited his disciples to be part of this project. Now they had an identity and significance untethered to their job or financial status. So they could walk away from it (if that was called for), or pick it up again, or approach it in a different way from before. They had a new freedom both *from* their work and *in* their work. Notice that when Jesus called them to follow him, it was at the moment of great financial success—the huge catch of fish. But they could, and they did, leave their nets behind. In Jesus's presence, they were no longer controlled by their work.

This may all sound very idealistic to us. After all, the sea wasn't going to run out of fish and there were no fisherman bosses who were going to block their reentry to the profession after their unpaid leave with Jesus. But the story forces us to ask important questions. Do we let our work control us to such a degree that we don't even notice when God comes through with a new opportunity? Do we get our "big catch"—a year-end bonus or next new job—and immediately start focusing on the prospect of the next bigger one? How can we have any freedom from the temptations of work and still keep our job?

A fascinating example of this freedom is found in the second book of Kings, chapter 5. After Naaman, the prime minister of Syria, is converted to faith in Israel's God, he does not abandon his job. Instead he takes a load of dirt from Israel to kneel on whenever he does his state duty of accompanying the king of Syria into the temple of Rimmon, the Syrian deity. Rimmon was basically a divinized version of Syria itself. So Naaman says, in effect, "I will still *serve* my nation, but I will no longer *worship* my nation. Syria's national interests are important to me, but are no longer my ultimate value or god." My friend in the private equity firm made a similar move when he waived his bonus from his organization's investment in a venture that was perfectly legal but did not help people flourish. For both of these men, an encounter with God had given them the power to break free of the idols of their vocational fields. This power freed them from the grip of the work beneath their work.

We have said that the gospel replaces the story that animates our work, it alters our conception of what work is, and it reorients the ethical compass we use for work. In addition to all this, the gospel also gives us new power for work by supplying us with a new passion and a deeper kind of rest.

The Power of True Passion

One of the words we read and hear about often today is *passion*. Passion leads you to excel in whatever you do. But there are dif-

ferent sources and kinds of passion. Sometimes it generates frenetic activity more grounded in fear of failure than in pursuit of
success. That kind of passion can produce a lot of energy, but
from a Christian point of view it is a counterfeit. It is fueled by
the work under the work. And it is unsustainable, like the extreme brightness of a dying lightbulb.

Dorothy Sayers helps us understand the counterfeit passion
that can drive our work. In her book *Creed or Chaos?*, Sayers addresses the traditional seven deadly sins, including acedia, which
is often translated as "sloth." But as Sayers explains it, that is a
misnomer, because laziness (the way we normally define sloth) is
not the real nature of this condition. Acedia, she says, means a
life driven by mere cost-benefit analysis of "what's in it for me."
She writes, "Acedia is the sin which believes in nothing, cares for
nothing, enjoys nothing, loves nothing, hates nothing, finds purpose in nothing, lives for nothing and only remains alive because
there is nothing for which it will die. We have known it far too
well for many years, the only thing perhaps we have not known
about it is it is a mortal sin."[208]

Sayers goes on to say that a person characterized by acedia—in
which their driving passion is for their own needs, comfort, and
interests—does not necessarily look lazy at all. Indeed, this type
of person seems to generate lots of activity. But, she argues, acedia, "the sin of the empty soul," opens you to letting all the other
sins be the motivations for your work.

> It is one of the favorite tricks of this Sin to dissemble
> itself under a cover of a whiffling activity of body. We
> think that if we are busily rushing about and doing
> things we cannot be suffering from Sloth. . . . Glut-

tony offers a world of dancing, dining, sports, and dashing very fast from place to place to gape at beauty spots. . . . Covetousness rakes us out of the bed at an early hour in order that we may put pep and hustle into our business; Envy sets us to gossip and scandals, to writing cantankerous letters to the paper, and to the unearthing of secrets and scavenging of desk bins; Wrath provides (very ingeniously) the argument that the only fitting activity in a world so full of evil doers and evil demons is to curse loudly and incessantly: "Whatever brute and blackguard made the world"; while Lust provides that round of dreary promiscuity that passes for bodily vigor. But these are all disguises for the empty heart and the empty brain and the empty soul of Acedia. . . . In the world it calls itself Tolerance but in hell it is called Despair.[209]

I find this point hits home as a brilliant exposition of idolatry. Without something bigger than yourself to work for, then all of your work energy is actually fueled by one of the other six deadly sins. You may work exceptionally hard because of envy to get ahead of somebody, or because of pride to prove yourself, or because of greed or even gluttony for pleasure. In short, acedia is the most subtle idolatry of all. It puts the cynical self at the center of your life. And when you do that you release all the worst vices and sins to be the main animating energies behind your work.

A main plot device of *The Lord of the Rings* trilogy is the corrupting effect of the Ring of Power. When you put on the Ring, it magnifies your own will to power; and in doing so, it turns you evil. In a number of places where one of the hobbits puts on the ring, the description says something to this effect: "When the Ring goes on, you become the only real thing. You are a little, dark, solid rock in a ghostly world. Everything else is vague and shadowy." In some ways, our contemporary culture operates like the Ring of Power, magnifying the self-serving nature of sin in every human heart. It tells us in myriad ways every day that nobody has the right to tell us what is right or wrong for us—that in the end there is no standard or authority higher than the Choosing Self. Our consciousness and our needs are more real than anything else outside us; there is nothing to which we should submit, nothing that may trump our own happiness without our permission; and there is nothing for which we should sacrifice our freedom. But in the Bible, the very definition of passion—think of Christ's Passion—is to sacrifice your freedom for someone else.

Romans 12 addresses this truth at a practical level. Paul starts this way: "I urge you, brothers and sisters, in view of God's mercy, to offer your bodies as living sacrifice" (Romans 12:1). Paul is using temple language; he's leading us to think about a worshipper coming with an offering. But he's not talking about a sin offering, where you've sinned and are now reconciling with God. Rather, he's talking about a burnt offering, which had to be a choice animal from your flock—a strong one, without blemish. The burnt offering was offered as a way of showing your absolute commitment to God, as if to say, "Everything I have is yours, with no reservations." In other words, it was an expression of passion.

In fact, the term "living sacrifice" is deliberately paradoxical because sacrifices were dead. That's part of what it meant to be a sacrifice. To say to God's people, "I want you to be a living slain thing," is meant to be a jolt; it's a way of saying you have to continually be in the rhythm of dying to your own interest and living for God. That's the passion God asks of you. What might this look like? The rest of Romans 12 spells it out, but there is one particular verse from the passage that puts a fine point on what it means to be a living sacrifice: "Never be lacking in zeal, but keep your spiritual fervor, serving the Lord" (Romans 12:11).

There are two specifics in this verse. First, the word "zeal" is the translation of a Greek word meaning a combination of urgency and diligence. It is possible to be frenetic—to be urgent without focus and discipline. It is possible to be plodding, or diligent without a sense of urgency. But God's charge means that you are to be both urgent and disciplined. Second, when the verse says, "keep your spiritual fervor," the Greek literally says, "as to your spirit boiling." So we are asked to bring emotion, discipline, and urgency to the task of being living sacrifices in the lives we lead and the work we do. We are asked to live with passion.

So where does this true passion come from? Paul starts the whole chapter with, "I urge you . . . *in view of God's mercy* to offer your bodies as a living sacrifice." What is it about God's mercy that, if you viewed it, would allow you to become a living sacrifice—into a person who died to your own needs, who stopped doing the work under the work, and who transferred your passion to God? The answer, of course, is Jesus, the ultimate living sacrifice and the ultimate form of God's mercy. When you see Jesus suffer and sacrifice for you, when his passion is burned into your imagination, it will become very clear whether the things *you* are passionate about are just forms of the other six deadly sins.

But why was Jesus suffering? Where was his passion and sacrifice coming from? In John 17, Jesus Christ looks at his disciples and says to the Father, "For them I sanctify myself" (John 17:19). The original word "sanctify" meant to set yourself apart like an

Olympic runner. We know what it means to train for the Olympics. It means that absolutely everything in life is subordinated to one goal. It means that every minute of the day, every activity is done in such a way as to contribute to that aim. There is a great deal of pain every day, but it is endured without complaint. Only that level of passion and commitment can earn the gold.

And so it was with Jesus and his passion. He set himself apart for the goal of our salvation. He lost everything, endured everything, to obtain it. Jesus Christ's passion was for you and for his Father—not for himself. There is our model. When the extent and depth of Jesus's passion for you fully dawns on your heart, it will generate passion for the work he has called you uniquely to do in the world. When you realize what he has done to rescue you, your pride and envy begin to disappear because you don't need to get your self-worth from being richer, cooler, more powerful, or more comfortable.

Instead of working out of the false passion of acedia, which is born of selfishness, you are working out of true passion, which is born of selflessness. You are adopted into God's family, so you already have your affirmation. You are justified in God's sight, so you have nothing to prove. You have been saved through a dying sacrifice, so you are free to be a living one. You are loved ceaselessly, so you can work tirelessly in response to a quiet inner fullness.

The Power of Deep Rest

There is a symbiotic relationship between work and rest. Of course we know this at one level. We get away from work in order to replenish our bodies and minds. Resting, or practicing Sabbath, is also a way to help us get perspective on our work and put it in its proper place. Often we can't see our work properly until we get some distance from it and reimmerse ourselves in other activities. Then we see that there is more to life than work. With that perspective and rested bodies and minds, we return to do more and better work.

But the relationship between work and rest operates at a deeper level as well. All of us are haunted by the work under the work—that need to prove and save ourselves, to gain a sense of worth and identity. But if we can experience gospel-rest in our hearts, if we can be free from the need to earn our salvation through our work, we will have a deep reservoir of refreshment that continually rejuvenates us, restores our perspective, and renews our passion.

To understand this deep rest we need to look at the biblical meaning of the Sabbath—to understand what it is a sign of, and what it points to.

> Remember the Sabbath day by keeping it holy. Six days you shall labor and do all your work, but the seventh day is a Sabbath to the Lord your God. On it you shall not do any work, neither you, nor your son or daughter, nor your male or female servant, nor your animals, nor any foreigner residing in your towns. For in six days the Lord made the heavens and the earth, the sea, and all that is in them, but he rested on the seventh day. Therefore the Lord blessed the Sabbath day and made it holy (Exodus 20:8–11).

> Observe the Sabbath day by keeping it holy, as the Lord your God has commanded you. Six days you

shall labor and do all your work, but the seventh day is a Sabbath to the Lord your God. On it you shall not do any work, neither you, nor your son or daughter, nor your male or female servant, nor your ox, your donkey or any of your animals, nor any foreigner residing in your towns, so that your male and female servants may rest, as you do. Remember that you were slaves in Egypt and that the Lord your God brought you out of there with a mighty hand and an outstretched arm. Therefore the Lord your God has commanded you to observe the Sabbath day (Deuteronomy 5:12–15).

Exodus 20 ties the observance of a Sabbath day to God's creation. "For God rested on the seventh day." What does this mean practically? Since God rested after his creation, we must also rest after ours. This rhythm of work and rest is not only for believers; it is for everyone, as part of our created nature. Overwork or underwork violates that nature and leads to breakdown. To rest is actually a way to enjoy and honor the goodness of God's creation and our own. To violate the rhythm of work and rest (in either direction) leads to chaos in our life and in the world around us. Sabbath is therefore a *celebration of our design*.

Deuteronomy 5 goes on to tie the observance of Sabbath to God's redemption. Verse 15 says, "Remember that you were slaves in Egypt and that the Lord your God brought you out of there with a mighty hand and an outstretched arm. Therefore the Lord your God has commanded you to observe the Sabbath day." God portrays the Sabbath day as a reenactment of emancipation from slavery. It reminds us how he delivered his people from a condition in which they were not human beings, but simply units of capacity in Pharaoh's brick production system. Anyone who cannot obey God's command to observe the Sabbath is a slave, even a self-imposed one. Your own heart, or our materialistic culture, or an exploitative organization, or all of the above, will be abusing you if you don't have the ability to be disciplined in your practice of Sabbath. Sabbath is therefore a *declaration of our freedom*. It means you are not a slave—not to your culture's expectations, your family's hopes, your medical school's demands, not even to your own insecurities. It is important that you learn to speak this truth to yourself with a note of triumph—otherwise you will feel guilty for taking time off, or you will be unable to truly unplug.

The Sabbath legislation in Israel was enacted after the Exodus from Egypt. It was unique among world cultures at the time. It limited work, profit taking, exploitation, and economic production in general. Every seventh day no work could be done in the fields, and every seventh year the field was to remain fallow and not be cultivated at all. This surely meant that in the short run Israel was less economically productive and prosperous than its neighbors. But it was a land of free people. In the long run, of course, a deeply rested people are far more productive.

We are also to think of Sabbath as an *act of trust*. God appointed the Sabbath to remind us that he is working and resting. To practice Sabbath is a disciplined and faithful way to remember that you are not the one who keeps the world running, who provides for your family, not even the one who keeps your work projects moving forward. Entrepreneurs find it especially difficult to believe this. They have high levels of competence and very few team members. If they don't put in the hours, things don't get done. How easy to fall prey to the temptation to believe that they alone are holding up their corner of creation!

But by now you must see that God is there—you are not alone in your work. Jesus' famous discourse against worry (Matthew 6:25–34) is set in the context of work. He chides us that the plants of the field are cared for, though "they do not labor or spin" (verse 28). He reminds us that we are obviously more valuable to God than plants—so we shouldn't "run after" material things through our work (verse 32). So if you are worrying during your rest, you are not practicing Sabbath. It is a chance to meditate on passages like Matthew 6 until deep rest begins to penetrate you.

We might conclude that the practical benefits of the gospel's Sabbath rest come to us only as individuals, as we pray and read the Word—but that would be a mistake. God also strengthens us through the fellowship of community with other Christians. So for example Paul calls Christians to "carry each other's burdens, and in this way you will fulfill the law of Christ" (Galatians 6:2). And yet we are told that Jesus will relieve the burdened (Matthew 11:28-30) and that we are to cast all our cares and burdens on God (1 Peter 5:7) who bears them daily (Psalm 68:19). So which is it? Are we to look to God to support us under our work and burdens—or to other Christian brothers and sisters? Obviously the answer is both, because it is normally *through* the sympathy and encouragement of Christian friends that we experience God refreshing us and supporting us in our work.

The Rest Under the Rest

Come to me, all you who are weary and burdened, and I will give you rest. Take my yoke upon you and learn from me, for I am gentle and humble in heart, and you will find rest for your souls. For my yoke is easy and my burden is light (Matthew 11:28–30).

To get the deepest picture of what can happen to our work after we meet Christ, look at this passage. When Jesus calls all people to himself, he says he knows we are "weary and burdened" and that we need "rest." But Jesus's cure for our weariness is a "burden" (verse 30) and even a "yoke" (verse 29)! The yoke or harness put on a beast of burden was a symbol of slavery and grinding toil. How could this be a solution to the problem of deep weariness? Jesus says that it is *his* yoke and burden—and it is the only one that is light. Why? "For I am gentle and humble in heart, and you will find rest for your souls" (verse 29). He is the only boss who will not drive you into the ground, the only audience that does not need your best performance in order to be satisfied with you. Why is this? Because his work for you is finished.

In fact, the very definition of a Christian is someone who not only admires Jesus, emulates Jesus, and obeys Jesus, but who "rests in the finished work of Christ" instead of his or her own. Remember, God was able to rest in Genesis 2, verses 1–3 only because his creative work was finished. And a Christian is able to rest only because God's redemptive work is likewise finished in Christ. When the work under the work has been satisfied by the Son, all that's left for us to do is to serve the work we've been given by the Father.

We said before that many people are doing "work under the

work." They are not merely doing the work that draws the salary—they are also working to chase away their sense of insignificance. But here in Jesus we find the "rest under the rest," the REM of the soul. Without it, all other work will be unsatisfying. You won't be able to relax, even when you are supposed to be resting. You won't ever be able to walk away from your nets, even for an evening. You won't be able to enjoy the satisfaction that God intended when he called us to the work he prepared for us.

A classic example of this contrast is in the film *Chariots of Fire*, in which one man ran in the Olympics literally "to justify my existence," while another man had such deep rest in Christ that he could miss a likely gold medal by not running on Sunday. The first man *had* to get a medal, because he was doing the work beneath the work. (And at least in the film, the gold medal wouldn't even be enough to give him the deep rest he sought.) The second man, the devoted Christian Eric Liddell, did not care in the same way whether he won Olympic medals or not. He was at rest. He told his sister that God had simply made him fast, and "when I run, I feel his pleasure." He ran for the joy of running itself, and to delight the one who gave him the gifts to do so.

Remember John Coltrane's quote at the beginning of this book:

During the year 1957, I experienced, by the grace of God, a spiritual awakening which was to lead me to a richer, fuller, more productive life. At that time, in gratitude, I humbly asked to be given the means and privilege to make others happy through music . . . to inspire them to realize more and more of their capacities for living meaningful lives. Because there certainly is meaning to life. I feel this has been granted through His grace. ALL PRAISE TO GOD.

Coltrane was once like everyone else. He had said deep in his heart, "If I get really good, if I'm successful, if people applaud and appreciate me, then I'll know I'm significant; I'll know my life is worth something." But that kind of inner dynamic does not usually produce the best work—or the deepest rest. As C.S. Lewis observed,

> You will never make a good impression on other people until you stop thinking about what sort of impression you are making. Even in literature and art, no man who bothers about originality will ever be original: whereas if you simply try to tell the truth (without caring two pence how often it has been told before) you will, nine times out of ten, become original without ever having noticed it. . . . Give up yourself, and you will find your real self.[210]

Something happened to Coltrane to reveal his self. One night, after an exceptionally brilliant performance of the suite, *A Love Supreme*—a thirty-two-minute outpouring of praise to God—he stepped down from the stage and was heard to say, "*Nunc dimittis.*" These are Simeon's words in Luke 2 after he had seen the promised Messiah. They mean, essentially, "I could die happy now." Coltrane claimed to have had an experience of God's love that liberated him *from* the work under the work *for* the sake of the work itself. He had been given God's power and had felt

God's pleasure.[211] Coltrane had stopped making music for his own sake. He did it for the music's sake, the listener's sake, and God's sake.

In the Christian view, the way to find your calling is to look at the way you were created. Your gifts have not emerged by accident, but because the Creator gave them to you. But what if you're not at the point of running in the Olympics or leading on a world stage? What if you're struggling under an unfair boss or a tedious job that doesn't take advantage of all your gifts? It's liberating to accept that God is fully aware of where you are at any moment and that by serving the work you've been given you are serving him.

This is what Dorothy Sayers meant when she urged us to serve the work. And it is what Tolkien was getting at in "Leaf by Niggle." When your heart comes to hope in Christ and the future world he has guaranteed—when you are carrying his easy yoke— you finally have the power to work with a free heart. You can accept gladly whatever level of success and accomplishment God gives you in your vocation, because he has called you to it. You can work with passion and rest, knowing that ultimately the deepest desires of your heart—including your specific aspirations for your earthly work—will be fulfilled when you reach your true country, the new heavens and new earth. So in any time and place you can work with joy, satisfaction, and no regrets. You, too, can say, "*Nunc dimittis.*"

Epilogue

Leading People to Integrate Faith and Work

Redeemer Presbyterian Church has made vocational discipleship—helping people integrate their faith and work—a major focus of its overall ministry for almost ten years. Our particular church community lives as "resident aliens" in a huge city that is about 3 percent Christian. Many people are struggling to hold on to their faith as they try to contribute in their work communities. Others want their association with Jesus to be attractive; they don't want to widen the disconnect between the church and the people of the city. And still others are brand-new to the Christian faith and don't have a clue what it means to be a follower of Jesus in their whole life, including work. The challenge is to deepen the faith and theology of our congregation as well as enable them to engage the city with the love and truth of the gospel. We've sought to help our congregation live out the gospel in all spheres of culture in a way that seeks "the peace and prosperity" (Jeremiah 29:7) of the city in which God has placed us.

The letter that Jeremiah sent from Jerusalem to the elders,

priests, and people of Israel who had been carried into exile in Babylon has been influential in establishing the purpose and the tone of our ministry. First of all, the letter makes it clear that the Lord God claims responsibility for carrying his people into exile in the first place. When facing the trials of life in the big city and the demands of a high-pressure career it helps to remember God's sovereignty so that, by definition, we can be sure we are where he wants us to be. Second, he asks his people to seek the peace and prosperity of Babylon "because if it prospers, you too will prosper." As a congregation, we understand ourselves to be a small minority whom God has called to love and serve the city, our professions, our workplaces, and our neighborhoods. We seek to draw others into a redeeming and renewing faith, but also to serve alongside those who don't believe as we do, for the good of the city and the world. Discipleship for resident aliens, or exiles, is different from discipleship in a culture in which the Christian faith is assumed and the goal is to draw people back into something the culture already tells them they should do. At Redeemer we call the former "exilic discipleship."

Redeemer also has been shaped by a deep commitment to the promise that the gospel changes everything—in our hearts, our community, and our world. In the words of Abraham Kuyper, "There is not a square inch in the whole domain of our human existence over which Christ, who is Sovereign over all, does not cry: 'Mine!'"[212] Our faith and work ministry has sought to explore the power and promise of the the Christian story to change, redeem, and renew every aspect of our work lives, our work relationships, and the world we touch through the work we do.

As we've attempted to lead people into a better integration of faith and work, it's been important to pay attention to who they are. Most are seriously career minded—seeking careers in fields such as law, arts, finance, business, education, healthcare, technology, government, architecture, or advertising. They are also young (average age is thirty-three), 70 percent are single, and they are early in their careers. After nine years, with more than 1,500 people involved and over 150 volunteer leaders, we have been able to identify some of the specific ways of thinking (stories or worldviews) and some explicit behaviors (practices or habits) that are foundational for our people to enable them to more fully live out the gospel in their work.

When leading a change it is helpful to think about where you are and where you're going. The left column of the chart on the following page lists various beliefs or ways of thinking that are the starting point for many people in our church. They are presuppositions that shape the story they live by, as we discussed in Chapter 9. The right column gives the corresponding belief that we teach, seeking to help them reshape the story by which they live. These ideas, when they become real enough to us, actually change how we think, feel, and act. Most of these ideas have been elaborated in detail in this book in far more elegant language; this list is simply how we capture these most essential mind shifts that move a person toward a fuller application of the gospel in their work.

Change from	Change to
1. Individual salvation	The gospel changes everything (hearts, community, and world)
2. Being good	Being saved
3. Cheap grace	Costly grace (awareness of our sin)
4. Heaven is "up there"	Christ will come again—to this earth
5. God is value-add to us	In God's providence, we could contribute to his work on earth
6. Idols of this world	Living for God
7. Disdain of this world	Engaged in this world
8. "Bowling alone"	Accepting community
9. People matter	Institutions matter
10. Christian superiority	God can work through whomever he wants (common grace)

Many young adults come to us from other cities and were raised in evangelical churches that limited their application of the gospel to individual salvation. A large part of our ministry is focused on broadening their understanding of the gospel to apply it to our communities (in the form of gospel-changed relationships) and our organizations, city, and culture.

Many faith and work ministries focus on ethics—how to be good, honest, and fair. As we explained at the end of Chapter 7, it is very difficult (and even incompatible with the gospel) to just strive to be a good or heroic person, like Esther. A focus on being good distracts us from coming to terms with our sin; and it is because of our sin that Christ needed to die. We want to help people understand that the more they can recognize their own sin, the more they will experience God's grace. A life of gratitude for being saved is far more pleasing than a life based on self-righteousness over being good. This leads us to the next point—that the price God paid for us was costly. As we contemplate the death of Christ on the cross for us, we are both humbled and motivated to give ourselves back to him in return.

The next two points also go together. A heaven with just our souls floating around is very different from one in which we're living in the most beautiful city we could imagine on this earth: a city in which our paintings of trees (see the Introduction) or our clever new tools are more perfect than we could imagine them in this broken world. This understanding gives importance to the materiality of our surroundings. It gives us the motivation to give our best to contribute to the flourishing of the world now and this kingdom to come.

Chapter 8 was about idols. Our idols block our relationship with God and make us proud. We try to help people identify the idols of their profession and the idols they use to cope with the thorns and thistles of life and the desperate peril of existence without God. Each time we strip away an idol we can turn to God, and our trust in him grows.

In our individualistic environment we have significant resistance to the biblical idea of community. Of course, everyone says they want community, friendship, and love. But mention the words "accountability" or "commitment" and people run the other way. We work hard to demonstrate how God works in and through community; he even created the church so that we would work to share his gospel together. We also are constantly faced with the excellence and the generosity and the love of the people around us who don't know Christ. "How can it be that the person I work with acts like a better person than the Christians I know?" We get excited every time a famous football or basketball player is revealed to be a Christian, as though that somehow puts us in the excellence club in the eyes of the world. It's challenging to seek to be distinctive in how we work through the power of the resources Jesus has given us and yet, at the same time, see hundreds of other people who don't have those gospel resources outperform and out-distinguish us. Understanding common grace is key to our humility and appreciation of God's sovereignty.

The last thing we want to imply is that a gospel-filled work life is one of ten key rules or ideas—that is the quickest way to become self-righteous and blunt the beauty of the gospel. But it has been helpful to us to have some of the ideas in this book boiled down to a few phrases so we can help coach people toward more theologically sound thinking about their lives at work.

Instead our prayer is that, in wrestling with who God is and how to relate to him, our church will grow in humility, love, truth, grace, and justice; and that our neighbors in the city will flourish because we were here.

Redeemer's Center for Faith & Work

In 2002 Redeemer Presbyterian Church reorganized to focus on five primary areas of ministry in New York City: Worship & Evangelism, Community Formation, Mercy & Justice, Church Planting, and Faith & Work. In recruiting me (Katherine) to create a faith and work ministry, Redeemer was beginning to develop a vision to renew the city's institutions of culture through the people of the congregation who were employed in vocations throughout the city. I was stunned by the enthusiastic response from the congregation. I've launched lots of new products or services in my life, spending months and huge budgets on advertising and promotion, but this time the phone started ringing before I was even officially introduced.

Redeemer's CFW (Center for Faith & Work) started with no budget but huge pent-up demand. In 2003 the congregation was approximately three thousand worshippers a week, a good portion who were new to the Christian faith. Many were early in their careers and struggling to keep up with the daily demands of their work, let alone live out their faith. There was a dearth of mentors or role models within the church community.

We held a series of classes, led by some elders together with me, on topics such as vocational decision-making, leadership, and theology of work. We wanted to explore what the Bible had to say about concerns facing our congregation on a daily basis and to better understand our community's needs. A survey of several hundred participants in the classes revealed that:

- 6 percent had shared their faith in some way at work
- 55 percent prayed about their work
- 50 percent of all respondents responded affirmatively that they struggle to balance or integrate their desires with God's desire for their lives
- Very few recognized any way their work itself contributed to society.[213]

In 2005 Redeemer was able to raise money through a church-wide capital campaign enabling it to build out CFW over the next five years. The mission is to *equip*, *connect*, and *mobilize* our church community in their vocational spheres toward gospel-centered transformation for the common goal. Each of the goals of equipping, connecting, and mobilizing is important to help people work differently in light of the gospel. Many groups of Christians gather to meet one another, but without common frameworks for thinking about their faith, the discussions remain shallow. Churches often view themselves only in the business of teaching, assuming that if they've taught it, their congregation will apply it. But the study of adult learning has shown that people change only when they *hear* the new thinking (so we equip them), can *discuss* it among their peers (so we connect them), and can *apply* it in simulated or actual situations (so we try to mobilize them).

We also look at our programs in terms of the number of people they reach and the amount of resources we invest. The higher the commitment made by the participant, the more we'll invest. Hence, we make a significant investment in our intensive, year-long Gotham Fellowship, which will serve forty people in 2012–13. At the base of the pyramid (as depicted on the following page), there are many in the congregation who can invest only a weekend for a conference or one night for a lecture. Many participants share the cost of these programs, albeit for a short-term commitment. A brief description of the programs developed by CFW can be found on our website (www.faithandwork.org), and some are highlighted on the next page.

Vocation Groups

Vocation Groups at Redeemer typically meet monthly and are sometimes supplemented with special speaker programs or social events. Each group is volunteer-led by a team committed to

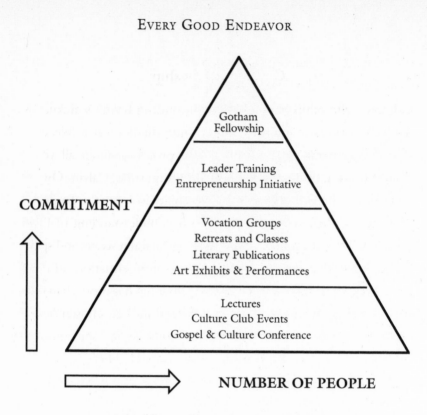

Figure 1

helping others in their profession meet, deepen in their faith, and explore the challenges and opportunities of their field in light of the gospel. The leader teams are innovative in their design of formats and topics. At the moment, Redeemer has numerous active Vocation Groups: Actors, Advertisers, Architecture, Engineering & Construction, Business, Dancers, Educators, Entrepreneurs, Fashion, Film, Finance, Healthcare, Higher Education, Information Technology, International Diplomacy, Law, Ph.D. Students, Visual Arts, and Writers.

Gotham Fellowship

Gotham Fellowship (named after Washington Irving's nickname for New York) is an intensive nine-month theological and leadership development program for young professionals in all vocations. Studying original sources such as Augustine, Calvin, Owen, and Luther, the Fellows grow in their ability to apply the gospel to their hearts, their relationships, and their understanding of their vocation. The program develops theological frameworks and spiritual practices that can be applied to the real-life situations of their work lives. In its fifth year, Gotham Fellowship has more than one hundred alumni serving in the church and in their chosen fields, who also continue to meet together periodically to "spur one another on to love and good works" (Hebrews 10:24).

Entrepreneurship Initiative (Ei)

Redeemer has been committed to serving New York not only by helping plant new churches to reach out to those who don't go to church or follow Jesus, but also by helping build an ecosystem of organizations and institutions that serve the city. The Ei supports entrepreneurs with a Business Plan Competition that invites early-stage entrepreneurs to think more theologically and strategically about their ventures. Winners are given a small grant and coaching from more seasoned entrepreneurs in the church community. The Ei has created a network of investors, senior leaders and coaches, experienced entrepreneurs, and early-stage entrepreneurs working together to serve the city with new gospel-centered ventures.

Arts Ministries

Between fifteen and twenty percent of Redeemer's congregation work in the arts—in music, theater, visual arts, dance, writing, design, and so on. Many artists in New York have felt particularly misunderstood or even rejected by the church because they are doing work that is not explicitly Christian, meaning directly for the church or containing an obvious Christian message. Our Arts Ministries engage artists in the theology of art and culture and provide opportunities for artists to share their work and collaborate on projects together.

Church-Based Discipleship

Redeemer and CFW believe that it is extremely valuable to have the faith and work ministry integrated into the life of the church. Many people have asked if we plan to spin it off into its own independent nonprofit, and the answer is "no." Our goal has been to model our conviction that vocational life is essential to being fully human in a biblical sense. Churches need to embrace the whole person—the married or single person, the healthy or ill person, the person at work and the person at home. Church-based faith and work ministry is important for two reasons: (1) work is often the crucible in which God shines a light on a person's idols and refines them in Christ-likeness, and (2) the church is touching the world at large through the faithful presence of its people in the workplace. The last ten years have shown us that faith and work ministry is so vital to the life of the congregation that it shouldn't be ignored. It draws in cultural influencers to become more shaped by the gospel; it provides the church a greater shared vision to serve the world; and it gives the church greater credibility in the culture in which it serves.

While most churches are smaller than Redeemer and would need to shape their ministry to integrate faith and work very differently, we encourage every church to develop something that fits its own context. Most churches could develop vocation groups to discuss the particular challenges and opportunities for workers in three basic fields: business, arts, and human services. Alternately, the pastor could gather a group of twelve to twenty-four people in different professions to read a book like Os Guinness's *The Call* or Al Wolters's *Creation Regained* and discuss its implications for their own lives. Redeemer has found that people are seeking far more theological study in order to navigate the challenges of their vocation, and they long for their pastor to be interested in learning more about the situations they face on a daily basis.

NOTES

FOREWORD

1. Rev. C. John "Jack" Miller was Senior Pastor of the New Life Presbyterian Church, which the author's family attended during the
mid-1980s. While this quote does not, to our knowledge, appear in a published book of Jack's, it was a frequent saying in his
preaching and teaching.

INTRODUCTION

2. Robert N. Bellah, "Is There a Common American Culture?," www
.robertbellah.com/articles_6.htm.
3. Robert Bellah, Richard Madsen, William M. Sullivan, Ann Swidler,
and Steven M. Tipton, *Habits of the Heart: Individualism and
Commitment in American Life* (Berkeley: University of California Press, 1985), 287–88.
4. For a good overview of the history of the modern "Faith at Work"
movement, and especially of its sources in the ecumenical, mainline churches, see David W. Miller, *God at Work: The History and
Promise of the Faith at Work Movement* (Oxford, 2007). Miller
recounts how several evangelical student organizations—
especially the Student Volunteer Movement and the World
Student Christian Federation (later the Student Christian

Movement)—shifted their focus in the early twentieth century away from evangelism and foreign missions and toward more social concerns. This gave rise to a number of new conferences and agencies, including the Faith and Order group and the Life and Work group, which eventually joined to become the World Council of Churches (p. 163, n.43). The 1937 World Conference of the Life and Work group in Oxford was particularly concerned with the impact of faith on work and economics. It was led by Joseph H. Oldham, who wrote that before the church stood "a great historic task—the task of restoring the lost unity between worship and work" (Miller, *God at Work,* 31). Most of the books written in the mid–twentieth century on the biblical view of work arose from these mainline, ecumenical circles, and the emphasis was on how Christian faith made work more sensitive to social ethics. These included Alan Richardson, *The Biblical Doctrine of Work* (SCM Press, 1952); *Work and Vocation,* ed., J.O. Nelson, (Harper and Brothers, 1954); W.R. Forrester, *Christian Vocation* (Scribner, 1953); Hendrik Kraemer, *A Theology of the Laity* (Westminster, 1958); and Stephen Neill and Hans-Ruedi Weber, *The Layman in Christian History* (Westminster, 1963), perhaps the only church history text highlighting the work not of ministers and missionaries but of lay Christian professionals working outside the church. On a more popular level, the works of Elton Trueblood were important, especially *Your Other Vocation* (Harper and Brothers, 1952).

5. In the mid–twentieth century a renaissance occurred in the church of lay-led small group fellowships. This movement had many branches—one was adoption of small group ministry by the newly founded post–World War II evangelical campus ministries such as Inter-Varsity Christian Fellowship, Campus Crusade for

Christ, and the Navigators. But perhaps the key figure was the Episcopal priest the Reverend Sam Shoemaker, who founded Faith at Work in New York City and later the Pittsburgh Experiment—two organizations based on lay-led small groups that included a focus on reaching people in the business world and having an impact on the workplace (Miller, *God at Work,* 32).

6. The mainline church understood the relationship of faith to work primarily as an effort to apply just, social ethics to capitalism— which was viewed with suspicion. Many conservative evangelicals were by contrast much more individualistic in their understanding of Christian faith. They were more positive toward market capitalism and so did not put their reform emphasis there. Instead their greatest concern was the need for personal decision and salvation. Therefore, to be a Christian at work meant primarily to evangelize your co-workers. Groups such as the Pentecostal organization Full Gospel Business Men's Fellowship, founded by Demos Shakarian, and the Fellowship of Companies for Christ, International, were distinct from mainline movements, since they emphasized personal ethics over social ethics—that is, working with integrity and honesty—as well as equipping people in business to evangelize their colleagues (Miller, *God at Work,* 51).

7. Luther, Calvin, and the other Protestant Reformers formulated their doctrine of work in contrast to that of the medieval Roman Catholic Church. The medievals saw human labor as a necessity for acquiring temporal goods of this life, but not of much use for achieving the eternal goods of the next life. So work was a peripheral matter. The Reformers, however, saw human work at the very center of God's purpose for human life. The Calvinists saw it as a way of continuing God's creative work of building a

God-honoring culture. Lutherans saw it as a vehicle for God's providential work of caring for his creation. But the Catholic theology of work did not remain static. Beginning with the encyclical of Pope Leo XIII's *Rerum Novarum* in 1891 and continuing to that of Pope John Paul II's *Laborem Exercens* in 1981, we can see a major shift. Pope Paul VI, for example, comments on Genesis chapter 1, verse 28, where God tells human beings to "fill the earth and subdue it," by saying, "the Bible, from the first page on, teaches us that the whole creation is for man, that it is his responsibility to develop it by intelligent effort, and by means of this labor to perfect it, so to speak, for his use" (quoted in Lee Hardy, *The Fabric of This World: Inquiries into Calling, Career Choice, and the Design of Human Work* [Eerdmans, 1990], 71). Many have pointed out the similarities between the Catholic understanding of natural law and the Reformed understanding of common grace, namely, that God gives wisdom and insight to all people, including non-Christians, so they can enrich the world through their work. In summary, today there is no longer a great divide between Catholic social teaching on the importance of work and that of the Protestant Reformation (see Hardy, *Fabric of This World*, 67ff.).

8. Much more on the contributions of the Protestant Reformers to our understanding of work is presented in future chapters.

9. "Leaf by Niggle" was first published in *The Dublin Review* in January 1945. There is some debate about when it was written. Tolkien's biographer Humphrey Carpenter believes it was written close to the time it was requested, in September 1944 (see Humphrey Carpenter, *Tolkien: A Biography* [Ballantine Books, 1977], 220–1), but Tom Shippey believes it was written closer to the start of World War II (see T.A. Shippey, *JRR Tolkien:*

Author of the Century [Houghton Mifflin, 2000], 266). The story can be found today in J.R.R. Tolkien, *Tree and Leaf* and *The Homecoming of Beorhtnoth* (HarperCollins, 2001), and J.R.R. Tolkien, *The Tolkien Reader* (Del Rey, 1986). These texts contain both "Leaf by Niggle" and Tolkien's classic essay "On Fairy Stories." The quotes from "Leaf by Niggle" in this section are taken from J.R.R. Tolkien, "Leaf by Niggle" in *Tree and Leaf* and *The Homecoming of Beorhtnoth*, 93–118.

10. This quote and the immediately following account of Tolkien's mind-set are taken from Humphrey Carpenter, *Tolkien*, 220–1 and 293–4.

11. Ibid., 221.

12. Quoted in Shippey, *JRR Tolkien*, 267.

13. Shippey cites the Old English poem "Bede's Death-Song," which begins, "Before the need-fare." A "need fare" was a compulsory journey, a long journey that all have to make, and it begins (Bede says) on one's "death-day." Ibid.

14. Tolkien, "Leaf by Niggle," 109–10.

15. Tom Shippey and Humphrey Carpenter represent two somewhat different interpretations of the ending of the story. Carpenter says Niggle's tree is a "true part of creation"—that is, it was there all along, part of the glorious true country of God. As an artist, Niggle was giving the world a very partial glimpse of this coming world, this underlying truth. Shippey is even more ambitious. He writes, "Niggle's reward is to find his picture *come true* [my emphasis] at the end of his journey, his 'sub-creation' accepted by the Creator" (pp. 276–7). In other words, Niggle's artistic imagination has been made real by God in the heavenly country as a reward.

16. Shippey points out that originally *The Dublin Review* asked Tolkien

for a work of "Catholic humanity" (p. 266). In other words, Tolkien saw his story as expressing a specifically Christian and Catholic understanding of creativity and art. Shippey points out that in the heavenly realm as depicted there is a "shepherd," obviously a reference to Christ (p. 277).

17. See the famous essay by Tolkien, "On Fairy Stories," in Tolkien, *Tree and Leaf*, 3ff.

18. Carpenter's words in *Tolkien*, 221.

19. Ibid.

CHAPTER 1—THE DESIGN OF WORK

20. Old Testament scholar Victor Hamilton writes, "God's creative activity is described twice as *his work*. The OT has two words for "labor." The second word emphasizes labor that is raw and unskilled. The first—and the one used here—designates skilled labor, work that is performed by a craftsman or an artisan. Such is the measure of the finesse and professional skills of God's work." V.P. Hamilton, *The Book of Genesis: Chapters 1–17* (Eerdmans, 1990), 142.

21. As many places in the Old Testament insist, the six-day workweek, with a day of rest for everyone, even servants and livestock, made Israel different from its neighbors. "In Egypt there was no day of interruption of the unending round of forced labor; Moses's requests for time to worship were met by Pharaoh with scorn; but Yahweh 'brought them out from there' and so commands them to celebrate the sabbath day as a "stopping day" proclaiming not only their dependence upon Yahweh but also their independence of all other peoples and powers. J.I. Durham, *Word Biblical Commentary: Exodus* (Word, 2002), 290.

22. A good, brief compilation of ancient creation myths can be found

in the *Encyclopedia Britannica Online* at http://www.britannica
.com/EBchecked/topic/142144/creation-myth.

23. Biblical scholar Gerhard von Rad has argued that, unlike any of its
neighbors, Israel could conceive of no divine powers on a par
with the Lord. Gerhard von Rad, *Wisdom in Israel* (SCM Press,
1970), 304.

24. See Hesiod's *Works and Days,* lines 109–29. The English translation
can be found online at *Elpenor: Home of the Greek Word,* http://
www.ellopos.net/elpenor/greek-texts/ancient-greece/hesiod/
works-days.asp?pg=4.

25. G.J. Wenham, *Word Biblical Commentary*, vol. 1, *Genesis 1–15*
(Word, 2002), 35.

26. Ibid., 34.

27. For more on this, see Chapter 3, "Work as Cultivation."

28. For more on this, see Chapter 4, "Work as Service."

29. Ben Witherington, *Work: A Kingdom Perspective on Labor* (Eerdmans, 2011), 2.

30. Lester DeKoster, *Work: The Meaning of Your Life* (Grand Rapids,
MI: Christian Library Press, 1982), 17.

31. Dorothy Sayers, "Why Work?" in *Creed or Chaos?* (Harcourt, Brace,
1949), 53.

32. For more on this concept, see Timothy Keller, "Is Christianity a
Straitjacket?" *The Reason for God: Belief in an Age of Skepticism*
(Dutton, 2008).

33. John Calvin, *Institutes of the Christian Religion,* ed. John T. McNeill,
trans. Ford Lewis Battles (Westminster Press, 1960), III.10.2.720–1.

34. Anglican hymn by William Henry Monk, "All Things Bright and
Beautiful."

35. Pieper, *Leisure,* 33.

CHAPTER 2—THE DIGNITY OF WORK

36. Ayn Rand, *Atlas Shrugged* (Penguin, 1999), 782.

37. Adriano Tilgher, *Work: What It Has Meant to Men Through the Ages* (Arno Press, 1977), quoted in Lee Hardy, *The Fabric of This World: Inquiries into Calling, Career Choice, and the Design of Human Work* (Eerdmans, 1990), 7.

38. Aristotle, *Politics*, I.VIII.9, and *Nicomachean Ethics*, X.7, both quoted in Ibid.

39. Plato, *Phaedo*, in *Plato in Twelve Volumes*, vol. 1, trans. Harold North Fowler (Harvard University Press, 1966).

40. Hardy, *Fabric of This World*, 27.

41. This is Luc Ferry's summary of Epictetus's teaching. See Luc Ferry, *A Brief History of Thought: A Philosophical Guide to Living*, trans. Theol Cuffe (HarperCollins, 2010), 45.

42. Leland Ryken, *Work and Leisure in Christian Perspective* (Multnomah, 1987), 64.

43. Hardy, *Fabric of This World*, 16.

44. Derek Kidner, *Genesis: An Introduction and Commentary* (Inter-Varsity Press, 1967), 61.

45. Alec Motyer, *Look to the Rock: An Old Testament Background to Our Understanding of Christ* (Kregel, 1996), 71.

46. V.P. Hamilton, *The Book of Genesis: Chapters 1–17* (Eerdmans, 1990), 135.

47. Phillip Jensen and Tony Payne, *Beginnings: Eden and Beyond*, Faith Walk Bible Studies (Crossway, 1999), 15.

48. Jeff Van Duzer, *Why Business Matters to God (And What Still Needs to Be Fixed)* (Inter-Varsity Press, 2010), 28–9.

CHAPTER 3—WORK AS CULTIVATION

49. Derek Kidner, *Genesis,* 61.

50. Some commentators point out that, even though Adam and Eve are told to "rule" over the animals and "subdue" them, Genesis chapter 1, verse 29 shows that this original dominion did not even allow them to kill animals or use their flesh for food. Only after the flood in Genesis chapter 9 does God give permission to consume animals as food. So "rule" and "subdue" cannot mean "exploit." See V.P. Hamilton, *The Book of Genesis: Chapters 1–17* (Eerdmans, 1990), 139.

51. Albert N. Wolters, *Creation Regained: A Transforming View of the World* (Eerdmans, 1985), 36.

52. http://www.tufenkian.com/about/james-tufenkian.html

53. Mark Noll, *The Scandal of the Evangelical Mind* (Eerdmans, 1995), 51.

54. You are doing what God has done, *if*—and this is a big "if"—your project does not add value to human life but only makes you a profit. The most obvious examples of things in this allegory are illegal drug dealing and pornography. But there are plenty of other projects—many coming to light in the recent recession—that made short-term profits for individual deal makers even though it was obvious the deals were not good for the institutions, for many customers and shareholders, or for society as a whole.

55. Andy Crouch, *Culture-Making: Recovering Our Creative Calling* (Inter-Varsity Press, 2008), 47.

CHAPTER 4—WORK AS SERVICE

56. Most of my biblical quotations use the New International Version translation of the Bible. Here I use the English Standard Version

because I believe it better brings out the sense of the original Greek text.

57. A point of controversy is that in verse 21 Paul denotes slavery as a "calling" in which it is possible to serve God. It is beyond our scope to enter into this discussion (though see Chapter 9 on our new motive and Ephesians chapter 6). It is important to observe that (a) in verse 21 Paul told Christians who were slaves to acquire their freedom if they could, and (b) we must not think that all slavery in ancient times was like modern chattel slavery. For an excellent treatment of this passage, see R.E. Ciampa and B.S. Rosner, *The First Letter to the Corinthians* (Eerdmans, 2010), 306–28. They write, "Paul has been careful not to make light of the circumstances of Christian slaves" (p. 327).

58. Ibid., 308–9.

59. Quoted in Ibid., 309.

60. Robert Bellah, Richard Madsen, William M. Sullivan, Ann Swidler, and Steven M. Tipton, *Habits of the Heart: Individualism and Commitment in American Life* (University of California Press, 1985), 287–8.

61. Ciampa and Rosner, *First Letter to the Corinthians*, 309, n.184.

62. See Louis Berkhof, *Systematic Theology* (Eerdmans, 1949), 569.

63. It is interesting to remember that Luther's other great opponents in the Reformation were the Anabaptists of the "Radical Reformation." The Anabaptists saw the public realm as essentially the realm of Satan and forbade their members to fulfill civil offices such as policeman, magistrate, and the like. Ironically, though the Anabaptists charged Reformers like Luther and Calvin with not rejecting the Catholic tradition enough, they had as negative a view of "secular" work in the world as did the Catholic Church at the time. Luther's (and Calvin's) teaching of all work as God's vocation therefore was set against both the Catholic Church and the Anabaptists.

64. Martin Luther, *Three Treatises* (Fortress, 1970), 12.

65. The translation of Luther cited makes use of the King James Version. See the translation by Edward Sittler in *Luther's Works: Selected Psalms III*, ed., J. Pelikan, vol. 14 (Concordia, 1958).

66. Ibid., 95.

67. *Luther's Large Catechism: With Study Questions,* trans. F. Samuel Janzow (Concordia, 1978), 90.

68. Pelikan, *Luther's Works*, vol. 14, 95.

69. Ibid., 96.

70. Ibid., 100.

71. Ibid., 96.

72. *Luther's Works, Sermon on the Mount and the Magnificat* ed. J. Pelikan, vol. 21, (Concordia, 1958), 237.

73. Hardy, *Fabric*, 45.

74. This is from his preface to the complete edition of Luther's Latin Writings (Wittenberg, 1545), printed in *Luther's Works*, vol. 34, *Career of the Reformer* (Fortress, 1960), 336–8.

75. *Luther's Works, Genesis Chapters 6–14*, eds. J. Pelikan and D.E. Poellot, vol. 2 (Concordia, 1960), 348.

76. *Luther's Works, Sermon on the Mount*, vol. 21, 367.

77. Dorothy Sayers, "Why Work?" in *Creed or Chaos?* (Harcourt, Brace, 1949), 51.

78. Sayers, "Creed or Chaos?" in *Creed or Chaos?*, 42–3.

79. Ibid.

80. Lester DeKoster, *Work: The Meaning of Your Life* (Christian Library Press, 1982), 5, 7, 9–10.

81. Sayers, *Creed or Chaos?*, 56–7.

82. Recounted in William E. Diehl, *The Monday Connection: A Spirituality of Competence, Affirmation, and Support in the Workplace,* (HarperCollins, 1991), 25–6.

83. Ibid., 29.

84. Ibid.

85. John Calvin, *Institutes of the Christian Religion,* ed. John T. McNeill, trans. Ford Lewis Battles (Westminster Press, 1960), III.11.6.725.

CHAPTER 5—WORK BECOMES FRUITLESS

86. Some have argued that Adam and Eve could have obeyed out of self-interest because God told them that if they ate it they would die—but within the context of the narrative they could not have been able to comprehend what that meant.

87. This section assumes that when Adam and Eve turned away from God, the human race sinned, and therefore you and I sinned as well. Romans 5:12 tells us that "all sinned" in the sin of Adam. This is counterintuitive to our individualistic Western society (though, it should be added, not to the rest of the world). One way Christian theologians have explained this biblical teaching is this: Adam was especially made by God to be our perfect representative. Therefore, we cannot protest that if we had been there we would have acted differently. Adam and Eve did exactly what we would have done if we had been there—and also what we continue to do in our own lives today. Thus we sinned "in them." See article on "Sin" in J.I. Packer and I.H. Marshall, eds., *The New Bible Dictionary, Third Edition* (Inter-Varsity Press, 1996), 1105ff.

88. William Butler Yeats, "The Second Coming" in *Michael Robartes and the Dancer* (Kessinger Publishing, 2010), 19.

89. David Atkinson, *The Message of Genesis 1–11: The Dawn of Creation* (Inter-Varsity, 1990), 87.

90. Alec Motyer, *Look to the Rock: An Old Testament Background to Our Understanding of Christ* (Inter-Varsity Press, 1996), 118–9.

91. This is a big subject. See Timothy Keller and Kathy Keller, *The Meaning of Marriage: Facing the Complexities of Commitment with the Wisdom of God* (Dutton, 2011), Chapter 6. Derek Kidner says that we see here in Genesis chapter 3, verse 16: "Love has slipped from the fully personal realm to that of instinctive urges passive and active." "To love and to cherish" becomes "to desire and to dominate" (Derek Kidner, *Genesis*, 71).

92. Albert C. Wolters, *Creation Regained: A Transforming View of the World* (Eerdmans, 1985), 44.

93. W.R. Forrester, *Christian Vocation* (Scribner, 1953), 129. Quoted in Ibid.

94. "Work, Worker" in *The Dictionary of Biblical Imagery*, eds. L. Ryken and T. Longman (Inter-Varsity Press, 1995), 966.

95. It should be observed that the real historical figures of Salieri and Mozart are not identical to the characters depicted in the play.

96. The script for Peter Shaffer's play *Amadeus* can be found at *The Daily Script*, http://www.dailyscript.com/scripts/amadeus .html (retrieved May 16, 2012).

97. From an interview with Sebastian Thrun in Andy Kessler, "What's Next for Silicon Valley?" *The Wall Street Journal*, June 16–17, 2012.

98. Crouch, *Culture-making*, 188. See also David Brooks, "Sam Spade at Starbucks," *The New York Times*, April 12, 2012.

99. Isaac Watts, "Joy to the World." In Isaac Watts, *The Psalms of David: Imitated in the Language of the New Testament and Applied to the Christian State and Worship* (London: C. Corrall, 1818).

CHAPTER 6—WORK BECOMES POINTLESS

100. Tremper Longman, *The Book of Ecclesiastes* (Eerdmans, 1998), 15–20.

101. Tradition has it that the speaker in Ecclesiastes describing his accrual of wisdom, money, and power is Solomon, the king of Israel after his father, David. There are major problems with this tradition, however, largely stemming from the evidence in the book itself. In Ecclesiastes chapter 1, verse 16 the speaker says, "I have increased in wisdom more than anyone who has ruled Jerusalem before me." But only David ruled Israel from Jerusalem before Solomon. It is highly unlikely that Solomon would have said this. See discussion in Longman, *Book of Ecclesiastes,* 2–9.

102. The Qoheleth character is not so much an atheist as a secularist, for whom God is vague and distant. But the author of the book shows at the very end that he is a man of faith who sees that life "under the sun" cannot be all there is. Though there are no exact parallels to the literary genre of Ecclesiastes in the Bible; the closest to it is the book of Job. There, too, a character is introduced in the beginning and evaluated at the end in a positive and straightforward way. In the midst of the book, the struggling central character says many dubious and self-contradictory things.

103. Peter Shaffer, *Amadeus, The Daily Script,* http://www.dailyscript .com/scripts/amadeus.html (retrieved May 16, 2012).

104. Michael A. Eaton, *Ecclesiastes: An Introduction and Commentary* (Inter-Varsity Press, 1983), 101.

105. Hardy, *Fabric of This World,* 31. On pages 29–37, Hardy gives a good overview and critique of Karl Marx's understanding of work.

106. Quoted in Ibid., 32.

107. See Peter Drucker, *The Concept of the Corporation* (John Day, 1946); *The Age of Discontinuity* (Harper and Row, 1969); *Post-Capitalist Society* (HarperCollins, 1993).

108. Derek Kidner, *A Time to Mourn and a Time to Dance* (Inter-Varsity Press, 1976), 47.

109. David Brooks, "The Service Patch," *The New York Times,* May 24, 2012.

110. Ibid.

111. John A. Bernbaum and Simon M. Steer, *Why Work? Careers and Employment in Biblical Perspective* (Baker, 1986), 70.

112. Dorothy Sayers, "Why Work?" in *Creed or Chaos?* (Harcourt, Brace, 1949), 59.

113. Ibid., 60–62.

CHAPTER 7—WORK BECOMES SELFISH

114. Kidner, *Genesis,* 109.

115. Kidner, *Genesis,* 110.

116. C.S. Lewis, *Mere Christianity* (San Francisco: Harper, 2001), 122.

117. Quote taken from the recording of a sermon by Dick Lucas, "Gen. 44-45: Story of Joseph Recalled and Applied: 4. No Way but down to Egypt." Originally preached at St. Helens Bishopsgate, London, on Wednesday, July 26, 1989.

118. See Raymond J. Bakke, *A Theology as Big as the City* (Inter-Varsity Press, 1997), Chapter 13: "The Persian Partnership for the Rebuilding of Jerusalem," 105ff.

119. Karen H. Jobes, *Esther: The NIV Application Commentary* (Grand Rapids, MI: Zondervan, 1999), 146.

CHAPTER 8—WORK REVEALS OUR IDOLS

120. Luc Ferry, *A Brief History of Thought: A Philosophical Guide to Living* (Harper, 2011), 3–12.

121. Martin Luther, *A Treatise Concerning Good Works* (1520; Kessinger Publishing Reprint, nd), X.XI.18–20.

122. See Timothy Keller, *Counterfeit Gods: The Empty Promises of Money,*

Sex, and Power, and the Only Hope That Matters (Dutton, 2009). Most of the book is dedicated to discerning personal and individual idols, but parts of Chapters 5 and 6 touch on cultural, corporate idols.

123. Andrew Delbanco, *The Real American Dream: A Meditation on Hope* (Harvard, 1999), 3, 23, 91.

124. The survey of Nietzsche's thought about idols and culture is found in Ferry, *Brief History of Thought*, 144–8. See Nietzsche, *Twilight of the Idols*, trans. Duncan Large (Oxford, 1998).

125. Nietzsche, the father of postmodern deconstruction, sought to outline a way of living that did not fall prey to "idolatry," but it is generally conceded that he did not. Many have pointed out that Nietzsche's relativism and "philosophy of the hammer" are basically truth claims. Ferry argues most convincingly that, in the name of smashing "idols," Nietzsche turns the real—the world as it is—into something essentially sacred. See Ferry, *Brief History of Thought*, 199–219.

126. Reinhold Niebuhr, *The Nature and Destiny of Man*, vol. 1, *Human Nature* (Scribner, 1964), 189. "The lust for power is prompted by a darkly conscious realization of its insecurity." See also "The most obvious forms of idolatry are those in which the world of meaning is organized around a center . . . such as the life of a tribe or nation, which is patently contingent and not ultimate" (165).

127. Steven Brull, "No Layoff Ideal Costs Japan Dearly," *The New York Times*, November 26, 1992, http://www.nytimes.com/1992/11/26/business/worldbusiness/26iht-labo.html.

128. Ferry, *Brief History of Thought*, 145–6.

129. Philip Kitcher, "The Trouble with Scientism: Why History and the Humanities Are Also a Form of Knowledge," *The New Republic*, May 4, 2012.

130. See Robert Bellah, Richard Madsen, William M. Sullivan, Ann Swidler, and Steven M. Tipton, *Habits of the Heart: Individualism and Commitment in American Life* (University of California Press, 1985).

131. Ferry, *Brief History of Thought*, 122.

132. Ibid., 126.

133. An example was Taylor's "Science of Shoveling" case study from his time at Bethlehem Iron Company (later Bethlehem Steel). When Taylor arrived, there were almost six hundred men shoveling coal, each having his own shovel and method. After thousands of hours of analysis, Taylor determined the most efficient shovel shape and the most efficient method of shoveling. After Taylor instituted these changes and tightly monitored workers every minute, the number of shovelers was cut by two-thirds, and the average number of tons shoveled per day per man more than tripled. Frederick W. Taylor, *The Principles of Scientific Management* (Harper and Brothers, 1911), 66ff. Cited in Lee Hardy, *The Fabric of This World: Inquiries into Calling, Career Choice, and the Design of Human Work* (Eerdmans, 1990), 132.

134. Quoted in Hardy, *Fabric of This World*, 139. See also the article by Stephen P. Waring, "Peter Drucker, MBO, and the Corporatist Critique of Scientific Management," Ohio State University Press, https://ohiostatepress.org/Books/Complete%20PDFs /Nelson%20Mental/10.pdf.

135. For an excellent, appreciative yet critical survey of Nietzsche's thought and influence, see Ferry, *Brief History of Thought*, Chapters 5–6, 143–219. The following paragraphs are dependent on Ferry's treatment.

136. See Edward Docx, "Postmodernism Is Dead," *Prospect*, July 20, 2011, http://www.prospectmagazine.co.uk/magazine/postmod ernism-is-dead-va-exhibition-age-of-authenticism.

137. Ferry, *Brief History of Thought*, 215–6.

138. Jacques Ellul, *The Technological Society*, trans. John Wilkinson (Alfred A. Knopf, 1964).

139. Delbanco, *Real American Dream*, 96–7, 102.

140. Ibid., 105.

141. See Wendell Berry, *Sex, Economy, Freedom, and Community: Eight Essays* (Pantheon, 1994); William T. Cavanaugh, *Being Consumed: Economics and Christian Desire* (Eerdmans, 2008); Richard A. Posner, *A Failure of Capitalism: The Crisis of '08 and the Descent into Depression* (Harvard, 2009). Posner makes the case against a major part of capitalist dogma, namely, that markets are self-correcting. See also Bob Goudzwaard, "The Ideology of Material Prosperity," *Idols of Our Time* (Inter-Varsity Press, 1984), 49ff.

142. Daniel Bell, *The Cultural Contradictions of Capitalism: 20th Anniversary Edition* (Basic Books, 1996).

143. Naomi Wolf, "This Global Financial Fraud and Its Gatekeepers," *The Guardian,* July 15, 2012, http://www.guardian.co.uk /commentisfree/2012/jul/14/global-financial-fraud -gatekeepers.

144. Nicholas Wolterstorff, *Justice: Rights and Wrongs* (Princeton University Press, 2010), 145.

145. Some readers will be interested to notice the connection between these four ways of integrating faith and work and the various theological "streams" that have shaped the Christian view of work. Chapter 9, "A New Story for Work," draws on the Reformed understanding of distinct worldviews and life views. Chapter 10, "A New Conception of Work," draws on the Lutheran appreciation of all human work as God's means to care for his creation and the human race. Chapter 12, "New Power for Work," accords with the

conservative evangelical focus on personal salvation and spiritual growth, while Chapter 11, "A New Compass for Work," aligns somewhat with the ecumenical-mainline emphasis on ethical behavior in work, and especially on social justice.

CHAPTER 9—A NEW STORY FOR WORK

146. Alasdair MacIntyre, *After Virtue: A Study in Moral Theory,* 2nd ed. (University of Notre Dame Press, 1984), 210.

147. For an accessible yet scholarly overview of how stories relate to worldview, see N.T. Wright, "Stories, Worldviews and Knowledge," *The New Testament and the People of God* (Fortress, 1992), 38–80. This material is very profitable and should be consulted for a good understanding of worldview and narrative in general, and especially as worldview is conveyed in the Bible through its narrative accounts.

148. Ibid.

149. A good introduction to the history of the concept and a compelling argument for its usefulness is David K. Naugle, *Worldview: The History of a Concept* (Eerdmans, 2002). See also James W. Sire, *Naming the Elephant: Worldview as a Concept* (Inter-Varsity Press, 2004). James K.A. Smith does not deny that we have comprehensive perspectives through which we interpret reality, and he heartily agrees they are in narratival form, but he argues that most people conceive of "worldview" today in terms that are too cognitive. He argues that your worldview is not merely a set of doctrinal and philosophical beliefs, which are completely formed by reason and information. It also comprises of a set of hopes and loves—"tacit" knowledge and heart attitudes—which are not all adopted consciously and deliberately. World-

view formation then does not happen only through argument or mainly through politics. Rather, it is the result of the narratives we embrace, especially those that give us a compelling and desirable picture of human flourishing that captures our heart and imagination. Those narratives are presented to us not only (or even mainly) in classrooms but through the stories we see, hear, and read from various cultural sources. James K.A. Smith, *Desiring the Kingdom: Worship, Worldview, and Cultural Formation* (Baker, 2009). Smith, citing Canadian philosopher Charles Taylor, proposes that the term "social imaginaries" would be a better term than "worldviews."

150. MacIntyre, *After Virtue*, 211, quoted in Wright, *New Testament*, 38.

151. Leslie Stevenson, *Seven Theories of Human Nature* (Oxford, 1974).

152. Ibid., 42.

153. Albert C. Wolters, *Creation Regained: A Transforming View of the World* (Eerdmans, 1985), 50.

154. "Two Murdochs, Two Views," *The Wall Street Journal*, August 24, 2012.

155. See Jay Rosen, "Journalism Is Itself a Religion," *Pressthink,* January 7, 2004, http://archive.pressthink.org/2004/01/07/press _religion.html.

156. Andrew Delbanco, *College: What It Was, Is, and Should Be* (Princeton University Press, 2012), 94–95.

157. C.S. Lewis, "Illustrations of the *Tao*," in *The Abolition of Man* (Collier, 1955), 7.

158. Andrew Delbanco, "A Smug Education?" *The New York Times,* March 12, 2012, http://www.nytimes.com/2012/03/09/ opinion/colleges-and-elitism.html.

159. A classic deconstruction of the art world as essentially a religious field with its own priesthood, doctrines, and temples is Tom

Wolfe's short 1975 piece of social criticism, *The Painted Word* (Bantam, 1975).

160. It is impossible to make a complete distinction between psychological and sociological idols, since all idols work on the heart, controlling us through fear and desire. And an internal idol such as the over-desire for human approval always works in close tandem with the idols of the culture. In traditional cultures the way to human approval is different than in an individualistic, Western culture. (Indeed the same behaviors that win approval in one culture are frowned upon in the other.) Nevertheless, the psychological idols always work intimately with sociological idols to form a unique "idol complex" that blinds and controls us. For more on this subject see Timothy Keller, *Counterfeit Gods: The Empty Promises of Money, Sex, and Power, and the Only Hope That Matters* (Dutton, 2009).

161. D. Martyn Lloyd-Jones, *Healing and the Scriptures* (Thomas Nelson, 1982), 14.

162. The quotes from doctors are from personal correspondence to the author.

163. Jerome Groopman, "God at the Bedside," *The New England Journal of Medicine,* vol. 350, no. 12, March 18, 2004, 1176–78.

164. Lloyd-Jones, *Healing and the Scriptures,* 50.

165. Christian Smith, *What Is a Person? Rethinking Humanity, Social Life, and the Moral Good from the Person Up* (University of Chicago Press, 2010), 203.

166. C. John Sommerville, *The Decline of the Secular University* (Oxford, 2007), 69–70.

167. See Rodney Stark, *For the Glory of God* (Princeton University Press, 2004); and Diogenes Allen, *Christian Belief in a Postmodern World: The Full Wealth of Conviction* (Westminster, 1989).

Notes

CHAPTER 10—A NEW CONCEPTION OF WORK

168. As noted previously, the worldview (work as creativity) approach tends to follow the Reformed or Calvinistic strand of the Protestant Reformation, while the providential (work as love) approach tends to follow the Lutheran. For a good overview, see Lee Hardy, *The Fabric of This World: Inquiries into Calling, Career Choice, and the Design of Human Work* (Eerdmans, 1990), Chapter 2, "Our Work, God's Providence: The Christians Concept of Vocation," 44–78. Hardy outlines the Lutheran, Calvinist, and modern Catholic views of work.

169. Richard Mouw, *He Shines in All That's Fair: Culture and Common Grace* (Eerdmans, 2001), 14.

170. Frances Hutcheson, eighteenth-century moral philosopher, used a famous illustration to demonstrate this. He asks us to imagine that we hear of a man who discovers buried treasure in his backyard—worth millions. But then you hear that he gives it all away to the poor. Even if you would never do so yourself, and even if you swagger publicly that such an act is stupid, you cannot help but admire what was done. There is an indelible sense of the moral beauty of the action.

171. Alec Motyer, *The Prophecy of Isaiah* (Inter-Varsity Press, 1993), 235.

172. John Calvin, *Institutes of the Christian Religion,* ed. John T. McNeill, trans. Ford Lewis Battles (Westminster Press, 1960), II.2.15.

173. Ibid., II.2.12.

174. From Leonard Bernstein's *The Joy of Music* (Simon & Schuster, 2004), 105.

175. Timothy Keller, *Generous Justice: How God's Grace Makes Us Just* (Dutton, 2010). See Chapter 7—"Doing Justice in the Public

Square," pp. 148ff. See also Daniel Strange, "Co-belligerence and common grace: Can the enemy of my enemy be my friend?" *Cambridge Papers*, vol. 14, no. 3, September 2005, http://www.jubilee-centre.org/document.php?id=48

176. This case study is heavily based on Ted Turnau, "Reflecting Theologically on Popular Culture as Meaningful," *Calvin Theological Journal* 37 (2002), 270–96. We will not go into the differences between popular culture and so-called "high" culture that Turnau explores.

177. For an excellent survey and practical description of these basic approaches to culture, see Andy Crouch, *Culture Making: Recovering our Creative Calling* (Inter-Varsity, 2008), Chapter 5, "Gestures and Postures," 78ff.

178. What does this "humble, critical" engagement look like? See Timothy Keller, *Center Church: Doing Balanced, Gospel-Centered Ministry in Your City* (Zondervan, 2012), Part 5, "Cultural Engagement," 181ff. Also see James D. Hunter, *To Change the World: The Irony, Tragedy, and Possibility of Christianity in Late Modernity* (Oxford, 2010.)

179. R.C. Zaehner, quoted by Steve Turner, *Hungry for Heaven: Rock 'n' Roll and the Search for Redemption* (Inter-Varsity Press, 1995), 1.

180. Turnau, "Reflecting Theologically," 279.

CHAPTER 11—A NEW COMPASS FOR WORK

181. Sheelah Kolhatkar, "Trading Down," *The New York Times*, July 5, 2009.

182. "Forswearing Greed," *The Economist*, June 6, 2009, 66.

183. Fred Catherwood, *Light, Salt, and the World of Business: Why We Must Stand Against Corruption* (International Fellowship of Evangelical Students, 2007).

184. "Why Was Transparency International Founded?" *Transparency International*, http://www.transparency.org/whoweare/organisation/faqs_on_transparency_international/2/#whyTIFounded.

185. Catherwood, *Light, Salt, and the World of Business*, 20.

186. Paul Batchelor and Steve Osei-Mensah, "Salt and Light: Christians' Role in Combating Corruption," *Lausanne Global Conversation*, http://conversation.lausanne.org/en/conversations/detail/12129#article_page_4.

187. See Meera Selva, "UK Politicians: Banking System Is Corrupt," *Seattle Times*, June 30, 2012, http://seattletimes.nwsource.com/html/businesstechnology/2018564970_apeubritain banks.html.

188. Hugh Heclo, *On Thinking Institutionally* (Oxford University Press, 2011).

189. Bruce K. Waltke, *The Book of Proverbs: Chapters 1–15* (Eerdmans, 2004), 96. My book *Generous Justice* (Dutton, 2010) expands on this concept.

190. See Lewis, *Abolition*, 95–121. Lewis lists eight traits that were universally recognized among ancient cultures, whether Northern European pagan, Greek and Roman, Egyptian, Jewish, Confucian, Buddhist, or Christian. These traits were general "beneficence" (namely, treating your neighbor as you want your neighbor to treat you); special beneficence (loyalty and love to one's own people, group, and nation); love and respect for one's parents and ancestors, care and concern for one's children and posterity; "justice" (including sexual faithfulness to one's spouse, truth telling, and equitable treatment of all parties in court); keeping promises; mercy to the poor and weak; and finally "great-heartedness," namely, courage, self-discipline, and honor.

As we will see in the rest of this chapter, the Christian "theological virtues" are largely missing. While ancient cultures required mercy for the poor and weak, it was not grounded in the teaching that every person was made in the image of God and therefore had a right to proper treatment. Rather, merciful behavior was seen as something that an honorable person did. In other words, mercy was something that was done for your own happiness and honor, not the poor person's. See how Augustine brought Christian doctrine to bear on ethics and changed the older pagan understanding of why and how to treat people weaker than you, in Nicholas Wolterstorff, "Augustine's Break with Eudaimonism," *Justice: Rights and Wrongs* (Princeton University Press, 2010), 180–207.

191. Thomas Aquinas, *Summa Theologica,* II.1.61. There are many versions available, including online versions. For example, see *New Advent,* http://www.newadvent.org/summa/2061.htm.

192. Luc Ferry, *A Brief History of Thought: A Philosophical Guide to Living* (HarperCollins, 2011), 58–9.

193. Ibid., 60.

194. For the most developed exposition of this understanding of why God created the world, see Jonathan Edwards's treatise "Concerning the End for Which God Created the World," in *The Works of Jonathan Edwards: Ethical Writings,* vol. 8, ed. Paul Ramsey (Yale University Press, 1989).

195. Ibid., 58.

196. Aristotle, *Politics,* I.V. The quote is from the translation of Benjamin Jowett (Dover Thrift Edition, 2000), 12.

197. John Calvin, *Institutes of the Christian Religion,* ed. John T. McNeill, trans. Ford Lewis Battles (Westminster Press, 1960), III.4.6.696–7. Here is the longer citation: "The great part of

[men] are most unworthy if they be judged by their own merit. But here Scripture helps in the best way when it teaches that we are not to consider that men merit of themselves but to look upon the image of God in all men, to which we owe all honor and love. [You] say, 'he is contemptible and worthless'; but the Lord shows him to be one to whom he has given the beauty of his image. Say that you owe nothing for any service of his; but God, as it were, has put him in his own place in order that you may recognize toward him the many and great benefits with which God has bound you to himself. Say that he does not deserve even your least effort for your sake; but the image of God, which recommends him to you, is worthy of your giving yourself and all your possessions. . . . You will say, 'He has deserved something far different of me.' Yet what has the Lord deserved? . . . remember not to consider men's evil intention but . . . look upon the image of God in them, which . . . with its beauty and dignity allures us to love and embrace them."

198. The main book is Brian Tierney, *The Idea of Natural Rights: Studies on Natural Rights, Natural Law and Church Law 1150–1625* (Scholars Press, 1997). Also see Tierney, "The Idea of Natural Rights—Origins and Persistence," *Northwestern Journal of International Human Rights*, vol. 2, Spring 2004.

199. While it is obvious that nonbelievers in God can believe in human rights and work very passionately for justice—indeed, this fits in with the Christian understanding of common grace—it is another thing to hold that their belief in human rights is intellectually warranted. Most secular people essentially share the beliefs of many of the older Greek and Roman thinkers, namely, that we sprung from an impersonal cosmos and after death our matter will go back to an undifferentiated, unconscious, impersonal

state. Yet secular governments and institutions do not return to the more logically consistent position that the ancients had and instead continue to hold to the inviolable dignity and value of each human individual. There is nothing that says they are not allowed to do so, and from any point of view, society will be better if they do not return to the older way of conceiving of human life. But such beliefs in human rights are an enormous leap of faith away from their own worldview's understanding of human nature, for belief in human rights makes far more sense if there is a God than if there is not. Nicholas Wolterstorff makes this case in "Is a Secular Grounding of Human Rights Possible?" and "A Theistic Grounding of Human Rights," chapters 15 and 16 in his book *Justice: Rights and Wrongs.* Also see Christian Smith, "Does Naturalism Warrant a Moral Belief in Universal Benevolence and Human Rights?" in *The Believing Primate: Scientific, Philosophical, and Theological Reflections on the Origin of Religion,* eds. J. Schloss and M. Murray (Oxford, 2009), 292–317. So while millions of nonreligious people believe in human dignity and human rights, such belief is essentially religious in nature.

200. I have combined the NIV and KJV versions in the quoted passage, as I prefer the way the latter translation handles verse 16.

201. The modern reader winces at the words "slaves" (verse 5) and "masters" (verse 9) largely because we immediately think only of the modern African slave trade, in which slavery was race-based, lifelong, and based on kidnapping. However, in the ancient world there were many "slaveries." There is good evidence that much of slavery was very harsh and brutal, but there is also lots of evidence that many slaves were not treated like African slaves would be, but lived normal lives and were paid the going wage, but were not allowed to quit or change employers, and

were in slavery an average of ten years. Prisoners of war often became slaves, and men could be sentenced to being galley slaves for crimes. A person could become a slave for a set period of time in order to work off debts, because there was no such thing as bankruptcy in ancient times. Often the result was an indentured servanthood for years until the debts were paid. To our surprise, slaves could own slaves, and many slaves were doctors, professors, administrators, and civil servants. (See Andrew T. Lincoln's discussion of ancient slavery *Word Biblical Commentary: Ephesians* [Word, 1990] in his Word commentary on Ephesians, 415–20.) In his survey, Lincoln says that no one in ancient times could conceive of an economic or labor structure without it. While there were brutal forms of slavery, the concept—indentured labor in which the laborer was not free to market his skills to other employers—was considered a given. Quoting another scholar, he writes that this was so accepted, "one cannot correctly speak of the slave 'problem' in antiquity" (Lincoln quoting Westerman, 415.) In other words, no one— not even slaves—thought the whole institution should be abolished. This is why Paul's letters do not aim at abolishing slavery but rather aim to transform the variegated ancient institution from the inside. As the scholar F.F. Bruce says about Paul's brief statements about the equality of slaves and masters in the first book of Corinthians, Galatians, Ephesians, Colossians, and Philemon, "What [Paul's letters] do is to bring us into an atmosphere in which the institution of slavery could only wilt and die" (F.F. Bruce, *Paul: Apostle of the Heart Set Free* [Eerdmans, 1977], 407). That is quite right. Slavery was an accepted institution in all cultures and societies of the world from time immemorial. Only within Christianity did the idea eventually arise that slavery was an abominable institution to be abolished. Why? Largely because of the implications of the gospel, laid out by Paul. All Christians are "slaves" of Christ, who himself came as a *doulos*, or servant (Philippians 2:7). Paul regularly told Christian slave owners that their slaves were equal to them in the sight of God and had to be treated as brothers (1 Corinthians 7:22–23). In Galatians chapter 3, verses 26–29, he writes that in Christ there is no slave or free—again, all are equal. The case study in which he applies this gospel theology is the book of Philemon. There Paul sends Onesimus, a Christian slave, back to his Christian master, Philemon. Philemon is told that Onesimus is his *beloved brother* in the Lord and a *fellow man*. In Miroslav Volf's book *Public Faith: How Followers of Christ Should Serve the Common Good* (Brazos, 2011), he says that this kind of teaching so transforms the master-servant relationship that, while it is still there in form—the servant is still to work for his employer—"slavery has been abolished even if its outer institutional shell remains . . ." (p. 92). This of course undermined and weakened the institution of slavery among Christians very quickly, so that it was "emptied of its inner content" until eventually it was discarded. Later, the institution of race-based, kidnapping-fueled slavery in the New World was so out of accord with biblical principles that Christians led the fight to have slavery abolished. Despite how complicated this subject is, it is important for Christians today to think it out. Many critics of Christianity simply assume that the Bible wrongly endorsed slavery and that therefore it may be wrong about other things it teaches. Actually, biblical theology destroyed the coercive heart of the institution of slavery within the Christian community and finally led Christians to abolish the inevitably oppression-prone institution itself. For more on how Christianity gave the world the idea that slavery was wrong, see Rodney Stark, *For the Glory of God* (Princeton University Press, 2003), Chapter 4, "God's Justice." In sum, when Paul speaks to Christians in Ephesians 6, he is not denouncing the institution of slavery per se (which would have been useless in imperial Rome). He is speaking directly to individual Christians within the institution about how to conduct themselves, and what he says is quite revolutionary.

202. P.T. O'Brien, *The Letter to the Ephesians*, Pillar New Testament Commentary (Grand Rapids, MI: Eerdmans, 1999), 454.

203. At the time Jesus was speaking, moths and vermin were a great danger, since garments were a major part of one's wealth; fashion changed little and clothing was often passed on to others— and, of course, human "thieves" are always out to take away the things we love most.

204. See Jonathan Rushworth and Michael Schluter, *Transforming Capitalism from Within: A Relational Approach to the Purpose, Performance, and Assessment of Companies* (Relationships Global, 2011).

205. Arlie Hochschild, *The Outsourced Self: Intimate Life in Market Times* (Metropolitan Books, 2012).

206. Some good places to start: On capitalism: Bob Goudzwaard, *Capitalism and Progress: A Diagnosis of Western Society* (Paternoster Press, 1997); John Medaille, *The Vocation of Business: Social Justice in the Marketplace* (Continuum Books, 2007). On business decisions: Jeff Van Duzer, "How Then Should We Do Business?" in *Why Business Matters to God: And What Still Needs to Be Fixed* (Inter-Varsity Press, 2010); Lee Hardy, "Part Two: Applications," *The Fabric of This World: Inquiries into Calling, Career Choice, and the Design of Human Work* (Eerdmans, 1990);

see also Rushworth and Schluter, *Transforming Capitalism from Within*. In general: Michael Goheen and Craig Bartholomew, "Life at the Crossroads: Perspectives on Some Areas of Public Life," *Living at the Crossroads: An Introduction to Christian Worldview* (Baker, 2008).

CHAPTER 12—NEW POWER FOR WORK

207. Dr. Ann, "I Do, Therefore I Am! Aren't I?," *Crosswalk,* recounted at http://christiannewsrssfeed.blogspot.com/2012/06/cross walk-i-do-therefore-i-am-arent-i.html.

208. Dorothy Sayers, *Creed or Chaos?* (Harcourt Brace, 1949), 81.

209. Ibid., 81–2.

210. C.S. Lewis, *Mere Christianity* (San Francisco: Harper, 2001), 226.

211. I should add that, while Eric Liddell was a Christian and Protestant missionary, John Coltrane's faith is not easily defined and some claim it was not specifically Christian. I am in no place to pass judgment one way or the other. Nevertheless, the connection that he expresses between God's love, our faith, and work is vivid and right.

EPILOGUE: LEADING PEOPLE TO INTEGRATE FAITH AND WORK

212. Quote from Kuyper's inaugural address at the dedication of the Free University. Found in *Abraham Kuyper: A Centennial Reader,* ed. James D. Bratt (Eerdmans, 1998), 488.

213. "Reflections on Work: A Survey," *Redeemer Report* (church newsletter, no longer available), January 2004.

ACKNOWLEDGMENTS

Katherine and I get our names on the cover of this book, but the quarterback of our team has been Scott Kauffmann, whose guidance and extensive editorial work has been crucial to bringing this book into existence. His long experience in the business world, his theological acumen, as well as his skill with words, all beautifully prepared him to lead us in crafting this work together. If you are finding the book helpful to you—thank him. As always, I am grateful to David McCormick and Brian Tart, whose editorial support continue to make Redeemer's growing literary production possible.

I also must acknowledge the impact of two particular friendships on my understanding of this subject. Mike Bontrager and Don Flow are two Christians in the business world who have embodied for me the faithful and joyful integration of gospel faith with their daily work. My job is to expound the Scripture and to make disciples, but without their examples—and their ability to disciple me—I would not have grasped as well much of the Bible's teaching about vocation.

Finally, I want to thank those to whom the book is dedicated—the staff and lay leaders of Redeemer's Center for Faith & Work—for living out the struggles and thinking through the implications of integrating your faith with your work. Because you are doing it, we can write about it. Under Katherine's leadership, the CFW staff—Kenyon Adams, Chris Dolan, Calvin Chin, Maria Fee, David Kim, and Amilee Watkins—have not just read and learned, discussed and applied, developed and taught a theology of work as outlined in these chapters. They have been willing to live it out together as they work—meaning they have looked at their own motivations, they have applied the gospel to their own hearts and seen it change them, and they have worked out of the joy that comes from a richer biblical appreciation of work. Our lay leaders, out there in the thorns and thistles of their vocations and industries, are wrestling with God over their own motivations and desires to see glimpses of him at work. They are being transparent to help others grow in their knowledge and practice. We commend you: Because you are doing it, you give evidence of the gospel—the good news of the coming kingdom of God—to the city in which God has placed you.

ABOUT THE AUTHORS

Timothy Keller was born and raised in Pennsylvania and educated at Bucknell University, Gordon-Conwell Theological Seminary, and Westminster Theological Seminary. He was first a pastor in Hopewell, Virginia. In 1989 he started Redeemer Presbyterian Church, in New York City, with his wife, Kathy, and their three sons. Today, Redeemer has more than five thousand regular Sunday attendees and has helped to start nearly two hundred new churches around the world. Also the author of *The Meaning of Marriage*, *Generous Justice*, *Counterfeit Gods*, *The Prodigal God*, *King's Cross*, and *The Reason for God*, Timothy Keller lives in New York City with his family.

Katherine Leary Alsdorf worked for twenty-five years in the high-tech industry as an economic analyst and in various executive leadership positions. After her CEO roles at One Touch Systems and Pensare, Redeemer Presbyterian Church recruited Katherine to lead the church's efforts in marketplace ministry, now called the Center for Faith & Work, which has grown to serve more than two thousand people a year. Katherine has served on the boards of International Arts Movement, Fellowship for the Performing Arts, and the Theology of Work project.

REDEEMER

The Redeemer imprint is dedicated to books that address pressing spiritual and social issues of the day in a way that speaks both to the core Christian audience and to seekers and skeptics alike. The mission for the Redeemer imprint is to bring the power of the Christian gospel to every part of life. The name comes from Redeemer Presbyterian Church in New York City, which Tim Keller started in 1989 with his wife, Kathy, and their three sons. Redeemer has begun a movement of contextualized urban ministry, thoughtful preaching, and church planting across America and throughout major world cities.